Scrubber

Scrubber

Mac Hardiman

with

Steve Pottinger

Ignite Books

2023

ISBN: 978-1-7394509-0-8

Typeset by Steve at Ignite.
www.ignitebooks.co.uk

Cover design by Alex Vann.
www.alexvanndesign.co.uk

Cover image by Nicole Lovell
www.nicolelovellphoto.co.uk

Printed and bound in the UK by
CPI Group (UK) Ltd
Croydon CR0 4YY

Scrubber

thanks to:

Margaret Hardiman for putting up with me
being away from home so much

Alison Dearden of Abbey Physio
for getitng me walking again

Matt and Elise Powell
for giving me my life back

Sharon Felton for the use of
Darlaston Town Hall

Steve Pottinger for making
this book happen

to all the wrestlers

Bedworth

Wrestling's been good to me. It's given me a living, it put me on TV, it's taken me up and down the country, and all around the world. This book'll tell you all about that, and more. And we might as well start at the beginning - or as near it as we can - with the question that will set us on our way.

How did I become a wrestler in the first place?

Well, I suppose it started all those years ago when I were working at the sheet metal firm and living in the bedsit with Marg. There was wrestling on once a month at Bedworth Civic Hall, and watching that was always going to be better than sitting in the bedsit watching the water run down the walls. So we started going.

That first time, we took Tina and Colin - Marg's kids - too, so it was quite an outing. A night out. Our treat to ourselves. We walked into the Civic Hall, up to the ticket office, and gave them our ticket numbers. Then walked on through to where the bar was, bumped into a couple who lived opposite us, on the other side of the road, and who owned a hotel, bought a hot drink for the kids and a pint for me - mine was always a pint - and got in our seats. We'd paid in advance to be sure of getting good seats. They were a couple of quid each, which was a fair whack at the time, but when you think you were seeing

TV stars, wrestlers you'd gawped at on Saturday afternoon on *World of Sport*, it were decent value.

The atmosphere was absolutely brilliant. And we were right in the front row. That first time we went to Bedworth, I think it was Rollerball Rocco and Marty Jones who was top of the bill, doing a ladder match. I'm not 100% sure, but that's what I remember. A ladder match, if you don't know, is where they hang something above the ring – a belt, or whatever – and the two of them will be wrestling each other to get it, trying to beat their opponent, fetch a ladder into the ring, climb up it, and get their hands on the belt before the other fella can stop them. This time round, I think the match was all about who would win the light-heavyweight championship. I do remember that Rocco cut his arm open on the ladder. Or had it cut open for him, to be more exact. Marty swung it round and it caught Rocco on the arm, and it sliced his arm open. They're sharp on the edges, them aluminium ladders, as I'd find out myself some years on – but let's not get ahead of ourselves. That night, having his arm cut open made no difference to Rocco, so far as I could tell, he just carried on, but Tina ran out because of the blood.

Later, Pat Roach were on against John Quinn. That ended up a proper mess. There was blood everywhere. I loved it.

And this became our treat. Each month, me and Marg would go to the wrestling. When we had Colin and Tina, we'd take them, too. And the more I saw, the more I got into it. I were fascinated. I'd always been into football, all the way through my childhood and teenage years, but this were just as good. Even though I were only watching, sitting in the audience, the adrenalin used to build up. I couldn't take my eyes off it. It were as if I were in the ring myself. It never occurred to me I would be in the ring one day - I had a steady job, and I'd just moved in with Marg, and how would you do that anyway? - but I loved what I was watching.

I was there at Bedworth Civic every month from then on. In the front row, so close to the ring you could see and hear everything, so close you'd feel the ring shake when one wrestler body slammed another. There was nothing like it. No spectacle came close. And that's how things might have stayed, but then the company I worked for, the sheet metal works, went into liquidation.

Suddenly, I needed a way of earning a living.

But before I tell you about that, let's go back to where and how it all began.

in this book you'll learn how I went from this...

to this...

Childhood

I were always a big lad. Always. When I was born on 10th January, 1955, I weighed 11lb 4oz, so I guess I started as I meant to go on. All my school life I were big, even though I did all the sports. I played football, cricket, swimming, everything. And I was still big. And if you think that by 'big' I mean carrying a few pounds, you'd be right. Still, it came in handy in the end, didn't it?

This big lad lived - with his mum, his dad, and his older sister - in a terraced house in Ansley Common, near Nuneaton. We moved there from Polesworth, which is where I was born, when I was about six months old, and I've lived in and around that area - in Nuneaton, round Nuneaton - ever since. All my childhood was spent in that terraced house in Ansley.

What was I like? Like most kids, I suppose. Just a bit bigger. And I hated school. Well, not all of it - I liked games, and PE, and I also liked the woodwork, and engineering. Anything that involved working with my hands. So, like I say, I loved engineering. But, for example, I hated French. Just couldn't get on with it. As soon as I walked into the French class, the teacher would take one look at me and send me out. Because I'd always play up, and there was nothing she knew to do about it. She weren't very old, and she hadn't a lot of teaching experience, and I'd play up, and she'd burst into tears. So it ended up that every time I went into the French class, she'd send me straight back out again, because that was easier for everyone.

As it happened, I got on really well with the woodwork teacher, Mr Holland, so she'd send me out and I'd wander on down to the woodwork room. He'd look me up and down, and say

You been chucked out of French again, Hardiman?
Yeah.

and he'd let me stay and help in the woodwork room. He asked no questions, and he didn't judge. Maybe he hated French, too, I don't know, but I really enjoyed spending lessons there, then strolling back to class. The French teacher didn't know where I'd been, and didn't care most like, neither. Then one day she chucked me out and said *Go and stand outside the headmaster's office!* I still went down the woodwork room to spend the session with Mr Holland, despite what she'd said. Now, in our school the coat pegs were square, and when I finished in the woodwork room, before I went back to the class, I held these pegs in my hand and squeezed really hard. They made two red lines across each hand, as if I'd been caned. I went back to the class and said *Look! I got that coz of you!* and showed her my hands, and she just burst into tears again.

Was I seen as a bit of a joker? No, not really. I liked a laugh, I still do. I just didn't like French. It'll be no surprise to hear I didn't pass the exam, because I didn't know half of what I should have learned. And when I say 'half', I probably mean a lot closer to 'any'.

Mostly, school and me didn't get on too well. But that wasn't all my fault. The school played its part, too. Like when I was at high school. Parkas with the fur round the hood were the fashion. I had one. Everybody had one. And then the headmaster decided they weren't suitable for school, and sent a letter round to parents saying we couldn't wear them. I showed my mum, and she sent a letter back saying

If it's raining, Mac won't be coming to school,
'cause he ain't got another coat.

One morning, I get up and it's chucking it down with rain. My mum says Put your coat on. So I put my parka on, and head to school. I get there, and the deputy headmaster drags me and my mate to one side – we're both wearing parkas – takes our coats off us, and flings them on the floor.

At dinnertime, I went home for dinner, like I always did. It had stopped raining, so not having my parka wasn't a problem, but when it was time to go back to school, it was chucking it down again. So I didn't go back. When my mum comes home from work at the hosiery factory, she says, *Where's your coat?* So I tell her what's happened.

Right, she says, *Come with me.* And she marches up to the school, and knocks on the deputy headmaster's door. At this point, you should know that he'd been at school with my mum when they were kids. She knocks on his door, he opens it, takes one look at her, and goes to shut the door on her. Mum puts her foot in the door, pushes it open, and gives him both barrels. You EVER take my son's coat off him and throw it on the floor - because it was still lying on the floor in his office - *You ever throw my son's coat on the floor again, and I'll pull you to pieces. I remember you when you were a kid walking round Hartshill with the arse of your trousers hanging out, and everybody taking the mickey out of you, so you don't do it to my lad.*

And with that, she picks up my coat, and my mate's coat, and walks out.

So I didn't have the best relationship with the deputy head, and I wasn't ever going to be any good at French, but life wasn't all bad. I absolutely loved football.

If I weren't in school, I were out playing football. I'd play till it were so dark you couldn't hardly see the ball. If it were too dark, or it were raining cats and dogs, and I couldn't be out playing football, I'd be in watching the telly. But otherwise, every spare minute was football. I played in goal, and I were good at it. When I was ten, a guy from West Brom came and watched me play - there was a bloke who lived round Ansley who were a scout for West Brom, and he got them to come and have a look - but they decided I was too big for them to take me on.

I kept playing, though. Saturday and Sundays - well, Sundays mainly - used to be all about football. Sunday afternoon we'd be playing a match, and as soon as that finished we'd all go up the Rec at the top of the estate and start playing again. That were regular, that were. As soon as the match finished, you'd change, go up the Rec, play football with fifteen, maybe twenty a side. It were great. Halftime would he as soon as one side had scored ten goals, so some days matches lasted till halfway to Christmas. You got your energy used up, that's for certain.

I liked playing football better than anything, but if I were watching it, I liked Manchester United. Right from being a schoolkid. Them and Nuneaton Borough. Never heard of them? Well, let me tell you, Nuneaton Borough weren't bad. I'd go to every home match with grandad George - my mom's dad, my dad's dad died before I were born - and my uncle Alan to watch them. I went down there once and they played Swansea in the FA Cup, and beat 'em. There were twenty-odd thousand there. It were heaving, it were. They wouldn't get away with it now. Another year they played Rotherham in the cup, and they drawed, so we had to go to Rotherham for the replay. My uncle got us train tickets to go, and then the morning of the match, the headmaster said *Anybody leaving school early to go to the football will be put on detention.*

Like that would stop us going to the game.

Detention next day were rammed. Half the school were there.

Home

If the weather turned bad, or it just got too dark to be out playing football, I'd head home. Our house was the second one in from the end in a row of terraces in Ansley Common, like a million other terraces across the country. But it was my home, and my world, and that was enough to make it special. I'd always run up the entry to the back of the house - because you never used the front door. The done thing were you come up the entry and in through the back of the house. The front door were only used if you had visitors. So I'd come up the entry and turn right into our yard. On the bottom wall of the entry, on what used to be the coal house, I'd chalked a set of wickets where I played cricket. And I think, if I remember right, the last time I visited the house, those wickets were still there.

So I'd come up the entry, turn right into our yard, and there was a bit of garden - lawn and flowers, and a fence round it - and then a long piece where, in years to come, I'd lay a board down to stand my motorbike on. I'd knock the fence down with that motorbike, too, but we'll come to that later. Then I'd barrel in through the back door and head through the kitchen. In my memory, it always smelt of cooking. When my mum were still alive, anyway. After that, not so much. But let's say that this day, when I come back into the house, my mum's at the sink, or stirring something at the cooker in the corner, or fetching something from the fridge.

Out of the kitchen into the living room, where there's a big Rayburn that were always kept alight to keep everywhere warm and heat the water. The cosiest room in the house. In the mornings, when I were a schoolkid, I'd come downstairs, my mum would have a big pot of porridge on top of the Rayburn, with the door open so you could see the fire, and I'd sit on her lap eating my porridge. If I need to warm up from being outside, this day when I come back in, I might sit myself in here for a while, but more likely I'll head through the living room and into the front room.

In there, is a radiogram, which were all the thing in them days, a television, a big sideboard, sofa and chairs. On the one wall, above the fireplace, are all my mum's brasses, and wherever we went we'd always buy her a piece of brass and she'd put it on the wall. In my memory of my childhood evenings, the fire is going - a coal fire with a log on it - and we're sitting watching the telly. I loved *The Sweeney, Starsky and Hutch, Steptoe and Son.* Mum used to like *Coronation Street.* And sometimes we'd watch *Crossroads,* and look out for the motel scenes that were filmed just up the A5, in Nuneaton.

I'm on my way up to my room, though, so I pass through the front room, past the the front door, and up the stairs. Directly at the top of the stairs is the toilet. At the side of that is the bathroom. And opposite the bathroom is my room. The small room, the box room. In there I've got a single bed, a big built-in wardrobe, my train set - a Hornby 00 on a hardboard base which is stood up against the back wall - and my Subbuteo.

There's no surprise that, being mad about football like I were, I had a Subbuteo set. I think that were the best football game that's ever been made, and you might think different, but you'd be wrong. And the chances were, on days where I were stuck in the house, I'd be playing Subbuteo, rolling the pitch out on the floor, and setting out the teams. Or setting up the goal and flicking tiddlywinks into it, which was the Subbuteo equivalent of kicking the ball against a wall when you've no-one to play with.

I had one of the early Subbuteo sets, where the figures of the players were cardboard. They had the same base as always, that little bakelite base, and you'd flick them to play, like you do now, but the figures were cardboard. Later, when they made sets with plastic figures instead of cardboard, you could paint them in the kit colours of your favourite team. I painted one lot of mine – probably in Man United colours, although it might have been Nuneaton Borough – and put 'em by the fire to dry. And the heat of the fire melted them a little, not much, but just enough so they were a tiny bit shorter than the normal Subbuteo figures.

Now, in our house I used to play Subbuteo on the floor because our table weren't big enough to put the pitch on, but a friend of mine had a table in their living room with it all set up. He even had the floodlights. And we had a league. A Subbuteo league. That's how mad on football we were. I took my ever-so-slightly-shorter Subbuteo team round to his, and my mate couldn't understand why I were thrashing him. By making them a bit shorter, it turned out they didn't rock so much. I'd changed their centre of balance, and made it lower.

It were an innocent mistake, but as soon as he worked that out, I were banned. I had to get rid of that team and use another one.

So, if I were outside, I'd be playing football. If I were inside, I'd be playing Subbuteo. Once in a while I'd get my train set down, and spend an afternoon playing with it. Or I might race my Scalextric, taking the pin out of the back so the cars swung a bit when they cornered - you either did that and know, or you don't - or I'd play with my fleet of army lorries, or my Corgi Chipperfields Circus. That was magic: the lorry with the booking office on the back, which towed two carriages with lions and tigers in, where the doors slid open so the animals could run free, and another lorry with a big crane for putting the big top up. I played with that for hours, making my own little world, and maybe it sowed the seeds of a life in wrestling, which is as near to running away and joining the circus as anything I know.

And at some point, when the very first video games came out, I had that silly tennis game. *Ping... ping... ping...* It must have driven my parents mad. I look at it now and think *I never played that??!! Surely I didn't??* But I did. We were easily pleased, back then.

I had football, and Subbuteo, and a happy home. And a family full of characters, as you'll learn....

Family

My mum were little but fiery. A redhead. She was very traditional, and she had that traditional attitude: *Don't you mess with my family.* If I were in the wrong, she'd tell me, and no mistake, but if I weren't - like when the deputy head took my parka - she'd stick up for me. And she were fearless. My dad was away working a lot of the time, so she was the one to take on school or teachers, and when she did, they knew about it. When I were at the junior school, I had school dinners. All the kids did. But I hated the custard. It were all thick, and like jelly. And this day, one of the teachers - because I said *I don't like the custard, I don't want it* - she spoon-fed me. Held me, and spooned the custard into my mouth, spoonful after spoonful. Mum went absolutely ballistic when I told her, and stormed off up to school to sort things out. I didn't eat any more custard at school after that.

Mum was one of four. She'd got two brothers and a sister, and they all got on, but her sister Bet and brother Alan got on best, and my mum was closest to Uncle Brian. I took after her, and loved him to bits. He was larger than life, a proper character who knew everybody and who everybody knew. The first thing you'd notice about Uncle Brian was he'd only got one arm. He lost the other in an accident when he was four. He'd climbed up the railway line, put his arm over to pull himself up, and a train come along. It chopped his arm off. He must have gone into shock. I don't think he even knew what had happened till he ran home, and my nan went to take his coat off and his arm came off with it. There was nothing they could do. His right arm ended in a stump about halfway down his upper arm, and he had an artificial arm fitted on it. And he never let it stop him doing anything. He was always heading off to sales and auctions, and whatever he bought, he'd bring it down to show my mum. Uncle Brian loved horses above anything, so a lot of the time he'd show up with some horse he'd picked up for a bargain.

I remember one day he said *I'm going to Coleshill sale, do you want to come?* And me and my mum headed off to Coleshill with him in his little mini van, the old sort of mini van with doors at the back. We're at the sale, and my mum sees this wardrobe. A small one, shorter than a tallboy. Just the thing for my room, she thinks, so she buys it. We get it to the van, and it won't fit in the back, and we haven't got a roof rack. So Uncle Brian puts the wardrobe on the roof, chucks a rope round the van, and ties the two of them together. This rope literally goes over the wardrobe and under the van, and we drive twenty mile back home, with my mum hanging out the window to keep hold of it.

He were more of a dad to me than anyone. I spent more time with him than my real dad, and it were always an adventure. But not necessarily a good one. Like when I were about thirteen years old, and he asked me to help train his dog, Simba. I was silly enough to do anything Uncle Brian asked, because I trusted him. He puts me in an old coat of his, gets some sacking, binds my arms up, and sets me off running across this field. Then he sends the dog, and the dog grabs me, pulls me down by the sacking on my arm. No problem. He kept letting me get a bit further and a bit further before he sends the dog. I says to him *You're letting me go too far. You can't get him off me till you get there, and it's taking ages.* Uncle Brian shakes his head.

Nah, he says. *You'll be all right, you'll be all right.*

I think he'd seen this kind of dog training on the telly. We practised it for weeks. Then one day, Alan turns up, and Uncle Brian decides to show him what a good job he's done of training Simba. So he puts this big coat on me, buttons it all up, wraps my arms up with the sacking, and tells me to run across the field. I knew what he was like, and I tell him *Don't let me go too far!* He says *You're all right, don't worry, don't worry.*

I set off. I run all the way across the field. There's no sign of Simba. I run into the next field, and I'm three-quarters of the way across that, and suddenly I hear the dog behind me. But the bloody thing doesn't grab me by the arms, it takes my legs instead, and they aren't wrapped up. It pulls me down, and it's biting my legs fit to bust. Well, Uncle Brian and Uncle Alan have got to run across two fields to get to me, and by the time they get there, I'm black and blue. My mum went mad at him. What did Uncle Brian say? What he always said.

Ah, he'll be all right, he'll be all right.

But that was Uncle Brian all over. Another time he had a horse, a two-year-old, and it weren't broke in. It were a Sunday afternoon, me and my dad had been up my grandma's, and Uncle Brian says to my dad *Me and you hold the horse, and we'll put Mac on it.* There's no saddle, bear in mind. No saddle. *We'll be able to hold it and it'll get the horse used to somebody being on his back.*

OK. Joe Soap here gets on the horse's back, sits there, they walk the horse round. It were all fine. I get off the horse, Uncle Brian says *Right, I'm going to take him back up the field now. You coming with me?* I says *Yeah, I'll come with you.* We get up the field and he says *Do you want to sit on the horse again? I'll hold him.* I says, are you sure? He says, *Yeah, yeah.* Well, he's put a saddle on this time. He chucks me up, I gets on, and he starts walking me round. He says *Here, hold the end of this rope, it's dragging on the floor...*

Stupid here, takes hold of the rope - the horse has still got no bridle or nothing - stupid here takes hold of the end of the rope, Uncle Brian goes *Whack!* on the horse's arse, and it takes off. I've never been on anything so fast. It doesn't want me on its back, and - truth be told - I don't want to be there. I see a hedge racing towards me, and I think *I am NOT going through there!* and I just pull my feet out of the stirrups and slide off the horse's back. I thought it had killed me. My back was in agony. I couldn't move. I'm lying on the ground holding my back, and Uncle Brian strolls over.

What did you jump off for? he says. *You'd have been all right.*

Uncle Brian

I could fill a book with stories about Uncle Brian and what he got up to. The things he done to me were unbelievable, but I loved him to bits. His dad, my grandad George, used to say to him *You'll kill that lad, doing these things!* Uncle Brian'd say *He's all right, dad, he's all right! Don't worry!* And most of the time - when I wasn't being savaged by dogs or falling off horses - I was.

It'd be tempting to say he had a rough life, but that's not true. Uncle Brian didn't have a rough life. He did everything he wanted, with his one arm. He played cricket, bowling with one arm, and won everything. He worked at the pit, and never had a day off sick in forty-eight years. He'd bike it to work every day - which was a good eight or nine miles - and when he wasn't at work he'd head off to the sales in Mowbray, Penkridge, or Coleshill. And if there were anything there that caught his eye, he'd buy it, whatever it was. Buy it, and sell it on. It weren't very often he didn't buy something and make some money on it. It might only be a pound, but a pound in them days, it was a lot of money.

He could turn his hand to anything. Woodwork. Keeping goats. Keeping rabbits. Tying wardrobes to the roof of his van for my mum. When Marg first met him, she was fascinated how he used to tie his shoelaces up with one hand. He was missing an arm, yes, but he never let it bother him, and he did more with one arm than most men ever manage with two. He loved gardening, and had three allotments. So he could dig them over, he got himself a rotavator. A big one, with six blades on the back. He had a piece of rope tied to the one handle, put over his head, and under his artificial arm, and he'd had all the controls moved to the left handle so he could operate them with his good hand. And away he'd go. And when he'd finished rotavating his allotments, he'd do other people's, too.

I've said before, he were more like a dad to me than my own dad. I learned no end of things off him. In his later years, when he'd finished working, he had a series of mini strokes. He didn't let that stop him. He just made the most of it. He got himself a sack barrow, and used it as a truck to put his stuff in so he could walk up and down the garden to the greenhouse and look after his plants. And I'd go up on a Sunday and mow his lawn, do any bits and bobs he needed doing. I were always with him. He were great and I loved him to bits.

Uncle Brian died four years ago, in his seventies. I were with him when he took his last breath. The things he did in his time were unbelievable. Anybody who met him, everybody who knew him, would tell you what a character he was. This next story is typical Uncle Brian. It sums the man up. And it never fails to make me smile.

One day, Roger, his brother-in-law says to him *Brian, you going to the sale?*

Yeah.

I could do with a ferret.

Right.

But I want a tame one.

OK, I'll see what's there.

Me and Uncle Brian head off to the sale. At the sale, there's a bloke with a sack. Uncle Brian points at it, asks the bloke *What's in that sack?*

A ferret.

Well, gerritout, let's have a look.

No way.

Why?

I ain't touching it, it'll rip me to bits.

I see.

Anyway, nobody bid on this ferret, so Uncle Brian buys it for a quid, takes it back to Roger. Roger takes the sack, stops a moment, asks Uncle Brian *Is it tame?*

Oh yeah, says Uncle Brian, nudging me with his pot arm so hard I nearly fell over *It's tame! The bloke had got it running all round him, hadn't he, Mac?*

Er... yeah.

Amazing wasn't it, Mac?

Er... yeah, that's right.

Roger puts his hand in the sack. I'll never forget it. He puts his hand in the sack, and the ferret bites right into his finger. Roger pulls his hand out of the sack, flicks his arm to get the ferret off, and it pulls a strip of skin off the whole length of his finger. The ferret goes flying across the room, hits the wall, drops dead.

Uncle Brian doesn't miss a beat. Says *You owe me two quid for that now.*

And he'd only paid a quid for it.

Mum

When you're young, you don't realise how much you're learning from the people around you, and especially how much you're learning from your family. But looking back, it's clear as day that the two biggest influences on me were my Uncle Brian and my mum.

Uncle Brian, well, he was a character, and more of a dad to me than my own dad was. My mum? She was the glue that held our family together. She'd be there at the Rayburn stirring the porridge when I got up in the morning, she made sure we never went hungry, she stood up for me against the teachers at school. She was the love that made our house a home.

Christmas Day when I was a kid and my mum was alive was just awesome. In the morning, me and my sister would each wake up to find our presents in a pillowcase at the bottom of our beds - and I don't know how my folks got them there without waking us up, because they never did wake us up - and this would be the one day in the year where we'd knock on mum and dad's bedroom door, wait for them to say *Come in!* and go in there to open them, together as a family.

One year, I remember, I wanted a bike. I really wanted a new bike. More than I'd ever wanted anything, ever. And there was no bike waiting at the bottom of my bed, no bike hidden in the pillowcase, I was certain of that. And I was so disappointed. I went in my parents' bedroom to open my other presents, and I were happy with the new football boots, and the new football – a proper one, a leather one that when you headed it, it tucked your neck into your shoulders – I were happy with all my presents, don't get me wrong, but underneath it all was this gnawing sense of disappointment that I hadn't got my bike. And then mum said

Will you go downstairs and make us a cup of tea?

I went downstairs, and there in the front room were my new bike. Well, I went absolutely crazy. I'd been disappointed and now I was even happier than ever. I'd had the low, and now there was the high. The way my mum had casually asked me to make her a cuppa, knowing I'd find the bike downstairs, it was absolutely fantastic. It was the best Christmas Day I'd ever had, bar none.

And Christmas Day was always good. My granddad, grandma, and mum's sister Bec who lived with them, would come round and sit down with the four of us for dinner. Then in the evening, Uncle Alan and Auntie Margaret and my Uncle Brian and Aunt Judy would come as well, and we'd all sit around and play pontoon, and for us kids it were a big thing if we won, because the grown-ups didn't let us win. We had to earn it. Well, maybe they did let us win from time to time, but not so as we noticed. It was a day where the house was full, and the coal fire would be on, with a big log on it, and the smell of the wood burning, and everyone – apart from Uncle Brian who didn't drink, but who might have a shandy – would be drinking bottles of beer, and shorts, and the house would be full of laughter, and the world would be perfect, and my mum was there at the heart of it all.

And then, when I were fifteen, she died.

She died of cancer. The doctors had kept telling her she just had hiatus hernia, but the weight kept dropping off her. She were only small to start with, but she went from nine and a half stone down to just five. She got to the point she couldn't keep any food down, except for one thing: chicken and mushroom soup from the Chinese in Nuneaton. We'd ring them every night, and they'd deliver it, and my mum would eat it, and we'd hope it might work a miracle. But it didn't.

It took six months for her to die. They finally took her in hospital and operated on her, but within six months she were dead. The surgeon said he'd rebuilt her stomach but the cancer was so advanced the rebuild would only have lasted 6-9 months and she'd have been as bad again. I thought at the time, although I missed her, it was better that way, better for her to be at rest than her being around for another few months and having to go through all that pain and suffering again. She'd kept getting fluid on her lungs, and they kept pumping it off, pumping it off, till she was so weak they couldn't do it any more. And that's actually the cause of death on the death certificate: fluid on the lungs. She were drowning, I imagine.

I'd tell myself her dying was a blessing really, because it was an end to her suffering. But it hit me hard. Really hard. Because I were all my mum. I never got on with my dad, I were all my mum. Whereas my sister was the other way, she were all my dad. So when I lost my mum it did hit me really hard, because I loved her. I missed her so much it was unbelievable.

I think it's fair to say I went off the rails a bit. I started drinking - properly drinking - and it all just went from there.

Drinking

I'd already discovered drinking.

I was at Hartshill high school, and a group of us used to go down the pub at the dinnertime from school, the Malt Shovel it was, and they had a little back room out the back and we'd go in there. There was about ten of us. We'd put our money in together and give it to the landlady and she'd do us sandwiches as well as serving us beer. The teachers were drinking in the front room of the pub, but they had no idea we were there, because we were in the back room and they never went through there.

So we'd regularly go down the pub of a dinnertime, and we only got caught out when somebody - and I'm not saying it was me - knocked a glass of cider over one of the other lads. We went back to school for the afternoon, he sat at the front of the class, and the teacher smelt the drink on him, and they sussed out what we'd been doing. We'd been doing it for about twelve months by then, though, and we'd never done any harm. We used to go down the pub, have half a pint or a pint, play darts, and go back to school. It were good. It were as much about the socialising as the drinking.

And then my mum died, and that left me and my dad in the house on our own. My sister had got married and moved out - she lived just across the road - and that meant there was just him and me. It wasn't easy. Our relationship weren't very good before my mum died, and without her there to soften the edges of him and me not getting on, and stop us butting heads, and with the house feeling emptier than it used to, things were always going to be difficult. I'd been all my mum, and now she wasn't there, and my dad was out driving lorries all day. Which was just as well, as we really didn't get on.

All my life, my dad had worked on tippers. He were in charge of sorting the runs, so he'd work his day shift and then he'd be in the office at nighttime, sorting the work out. That's what he said, anyway. Whether it were true... that's another story. According to him, he was always at work, or supposedly at work. All I know is that when I were a kid, we never seen him. He were out six, seven days a week. He'd do his job and then Saturdays and Sundays he'd be in the office sorting work out. That was his claim. But the truth? I think he was messing about. I know that leading up to the time my mum died, he were messing about with my sister's friend. He wasn't a drinker, he didn't drink hardly, but he couldn't keep his hands to himself. I think my mum had realised this before she died, too. I can't imagine how that made her feel. I do know how it made me feel.

What did I do? I kept getting into fights. I played football, and I got into fights.

I was good enough at both.

I was already playing amateur football. I'd started when I was fifteen, and I had to get permission off the headmaster to say I could play. The older guys on the team looked after me. As I got bigger and older, I learned to look after myself. But what they showed me, rubbed off. And what they showed me backed up what Uncle Brian had showed me, which was that if a fight came your way, you made sure you got your punch in before the other fella.

Uncle Brian ran a football team in the Sunday league, called Ansley Common. One Sunday - I were about eleven - Uncle Brian talked me into playing for them. I was out on the rec having a kick about, and he called me over.

We're short. Will you play?
I ain't got no boots.
You'll be all right.
My mam'll go mad.
Don't worry.

Uncle Brian's two stock phrases, right there. *You'll be all right. Don't worry.* I should have known then it was going to be trouble. The match were at a place called Pawsland in Nuneaton, which had five or six football pitches, and a row of sheds down the driveway to the fields where everybody got changed. I get changed, the match starts, and this bloke kicks me. Hard. I thought he'd broke my leg.

My Uncle Brian went mad. He said to one of the lads *Give them a corner.* The lad does. And Brian marks the guy who kicked me. The corner come over, Uncle Brian goes up against this bloke to head the ball, spins round, and hits the bloke straight under the chin with his pot arm. You could hear the crack all round the pitch, because it was a solid thing, his arm. The bloke goes down like a sack of spuds. Spark out he was. As he starts to come round, Uncle Brian leans in and says

That'll teach you to kick my nephew, won't it?

That were Uncle Brian showing me how to deal with trouble.

From then on, the committee in charge of the Sunday league said Brian had a choice: he either took his arm off before he played, or he had it taped down, but no way were they leaving him free to use it to knock other players out. Uncle Brian listened to their ultimatum, and said No. So he packed in playing, and from then on he just managed the team. It were all water off a duck's back to him.

And now I was fifteen, coming on sixteen, and ending up in a fight was easy. People would always try it on because I were big. And I'd seen from Uncle Brian how to deal with that. So I dealt with it. And as soon as I was sixteen, the moment it was my sixteenth birthday, I left school. I hadn't wanted to be there for ages, I was never going to learn French, and there was nothing they could teach me. So I left.

I left and started work at Peter Morton's, a woodworking place that made school furniture. I was supposed to be on an apprenticeship, but they told me I'd have to wait a little while before I could start that, and in the meantime could I go out with the lorry driver to deliver the furniture to schools instead? It meant I wouldn't be learning anything about woodworking, which was bad, but on the plus side my first wage packet was £2 10s for a whole week. And a pint of beer was only 11d.

Now I was earning, my dad asked me if I wanted to pay board. I could do that, or I could hand him my wages and have him give me some spending money back while he covered the cost of any new clothes or whatever I might need. I decided I'd hand him my wages. That first week I had to get a new shirt, and that cost him £3, and then he had to give me my spending money to last the end of the week on top of that, so he ended up out of pocket. The way I saw it, that was the luck of the draw. I wouldn't have new clothes every week, but if I knew he was paying, I wouldn't go short either. And whatever happened, I still had money to go out at the weekends. I was happy with that.

Life was simple. I lived at home with my dad, I played football, I got into fights, I got drunk at weekends. I missed my mum.

Work

The job at Peter Morton's didn't last long.

I'd been out on deliveries with the driver, helping him drop off orders at schools and businesses all round Nuneaton, but as far as I was concerned I was only doing this while I waited to start my apprenticeship. Yes, it was good to be working, and have money in my pocket, and be able to go out drinking of an evening and a weekend, but what I was looking forward to was working with wood, and learning how to make the furniture I was delivering. Then, six or seven months in, when the time came to sign up as an apprentice, the managers turned round and said

We aren't doing apprenticeships this year.

I'm not one for being treated like a mug. I never have been, and I never will be. So I walked out. I'd not got a job to walk out to, but no way was I staying in a place where I was being taken advantage of. Anyway, this was still a time when you could walk out of one job and be pretty much guaranteed of finding another, and that's what I did. I finished at Peter Morton's and got myself another job at Walter's Transport - up Plough Hill Road in Galley Common - working with the mechanic there, learning how to fix the lorries, finding out how to strip down and rebuild the engines. I got quite good at it, too, because the mechanic would let me learn something by doing it myself, and I've always learned best that way.

He'd show me how to do something, then leave me to have a go at it myself, at my own pace, while he went and did something else. Left to do things at my own pace, I'd learn a whole load faster than if he was standing there looking over my shoulder, and he understood that.

All my life I've always been keen to learn, and to try new things. Except maybe French, of course. You try something new, and you never know where it might take you, what doors it might open, how it might stop you from being bored. I'd been at Walter's Transport maybe a year when Les the boss got the chance to put one of his lorries in to Man-Able's quarry down Hartshill on day work. Because it would be in the quarry on day work, it wouldn't be driving on the public highway, which meant whoever drove it wouldn't need to have a driving licence.

I didn't have a driving licence.

As far as I was concerned, that meant I was the perfect candidate for the job, so when Les asked me if I wanted to spend my time driving a lorry round the quarry, I said *Yeah, of course I will.* And that's what I did. Learning by doing, again. I drove round the quarry all day, every day, and the only time I had to cross a public road was if I were running down to the railway sidings, and everybody was happy to turn a blind eye to that, for a while at least. Monday to Friday I drove the lorry round the quarry, and then on Friday evening, if it needed any work doing, they'd tow me back to the yard which was about six miles away, and then we'd tow it back to the quarry for Monday morning. Yes, it would be better - and a little bit more legal - if I had a driving licence, but seeing as that involved booking lessons and paying for them, and I was more interested in spending my free time playing football and drinking, I didn't see how that would ever happen.

Then, luckily for me, Walter's had a lorry tip over. It had been carrying a load of steel bales on, and they slipped, and the chassis tipped over. Happily for the driver, the cab stayed upright and on the road, but the chassis was badly twisted. The truck needed to go back to Rubery Owen to be repaired, and from the cab back we had to strip every last thing off the truck - every nut and bolt, the axles, every inch of the wiring - so they could repair it. We stripped it, we sent it off, Rubery Owen straightened it, and the truck came back.

Now, when the truck came back the actual fitter was off, so it was me, Les, and his son Keith who got given the job of putting it back together. Les had to come with us because neither Keith nor me could drive - officially and legally, anyway - and he was the only one with a licence. We cracked on with rebuilding the truck, and then it come to the re-wiring. Keith volunteered.

I'll do that! I'll do that!
OK, carry on...

But he couldn't do it. He couldn't get it right. Eventually, Les turns to me. *Will you have a go?* he asks. He wasn't a stupid man, and I reckon he knew I'd be up for the challenge. I says *I'll have a go, if you just leave me alone with the book, and I'll do it myself.*

Les nods.

OK, he says, *we'll do that. And if you can do it, I'll pay for you to learn to drive.*

I was coming up on eighteen years old by then. I sat myself down with the book, and the truck, and the wiring, and I set about getting it done. I did it in my own time, and at my own pace, and when I finished and the last piece of wiring was put in place, everything worked. It was absolutely spot on.

And fair play to Les, he kept his word, and paid for me to learn to drive. I had some lessons, and I took the test. I failed the first time, but the second time I passed. That was it. I were away then. If one of Walter's trucks broke down and the fitter weren't about, I could go out on my own and fix it. I was on decent money, too. I took my motorbike test and passed that, and bought myself a little motorbike, a Suzuki 125, second-hand. I had a job, a bike, money in my pocket, and beer and football at weekends.

Life was good. It was definitely good.

Arrangement

What made life even better was that my dad and I had come to an arrangement, an understanding of how to live in the same home and dance round each other without things all blowing up.

Firstly, I took on the cooking. I enjoyed it and I were better at it than my dad, who was best kept out of the kitchen at all costs. By comparison, I weren't a bad cook. As a kid, I'd watched how my mum put together a proper dinner, so now I'd come back from work, cook myself a good square meal, sit down and enjoy it, and then - because dad were a lorry driver, and didn't always know what time he'd be back - his dinner went in the oven.

I also did my own washing. Immediately after my mum died, my sister had been washing everything over the road at hers, but she were absolutely useless. Whatever it was she did to the clothes, I don't know. They'd come back the wrong colour. Or shrunk. So I took that over, too.

Mainly, though, the arrangement that me and my dad came to was that we kept out of each other's way. I still hadn't forgiven him for how he'd behaved when my mum were dying. I got up, I went to work, I came home, cooked, and went out. I had some good friends around me. There was a little group of mates I'd met playing football for Haunchwood, and whenever we finished playing football we'd be straight down the club. They'd open the back door for us, and we'd be there till kicking out time. Celebrating if we'd won, drowning our sorrows if we'd lost, so whatever happened we'd got an excuse. Either way, we were covered.

On weekends, I'd go out on Friday night and not come back till Sunday. It were good fun, but it also kept me away from him. I'd meet up with my mates, we'd go down the club at Galley Common, get in there as soon as it opened, come out at two in the morning, take some booze back to a mate's house, drink more, and I'd fall asleep on their sofa. Get some kip, and be back down the club again first thing next morning. I'd spend weekends drinking and sofa-surfing. One New Year I went missing for five days. I can't be sure about what happened... but I know it were good.

There was a lot of drinking. And I thought nothing of getting on my motorbike, however much I'd had. How I weren't killed on it, I don't know, because I got on it in some right states. We'd be in the club all night, drinking, then we'd go back to my mate's where I'd left the bike, and I'd weave my way up to Ansley village to the chip shop to get fish and chips for everyone. Sometimes, I'd have someone riding pillion so they could carry the orders back. Occasionally, they even had a helmet. We'd grab the orders, turn the bike round, and ride the mile and a half back to my mate's. We'd scoff the fish and chips, have some more drink, and I'd finish the night by riding the motorbike four miles home.

Mostly, that went well. Sometimes, it didn't. One night we came out the chip shop, set off, and I couldn't get any speed up at all. I thought *This motorbike ain't going very well...*

Then my mate tapped me on the shoulder, and says
I think you'd better stop.
Why?
My shoe's stuck in the back wheel.

He'd got his foot caught in the back wheel, managed to part free himself so he wasn't injured, but the wheel had chopped the back clean off his shoe, and it was stuck in the wheel. We levered it out, set off again, took everyone their fish and chips, had a laugh about it. We were young. That's what you do. But looking back, it wasn't the brightest move. it was a miracle I never got killed on that bike. It's less of a surprise I ended up losing my licence, but that was a few years off, yet, and for now I still believed I could get away with anything, and it'd all be OK. One night, my mate - the same guy who'd got his shoe caught in the wheel - asks me for a lift home, because he lived on the way to where I lived. He's too drunk to want to walk. And I'm too drunk to ride, but I tell him *Of course I will.*

I gets the bike out, we say ta-ra to everyone, and I set off. I get to his place, stop to let him off and think to myself *I wonder where he is...*

He weren't on there. So I carry on home. Next night we're down the club and he says

You're a bright one, ain't ya?
Why?
You said you'd give me a lift home.
I know.

And?

I stopped for you to get off, and you weren't there.

That's because I didn't even get on.

Oh.

You took off before I'd picked my feet up.

Oh.

I was standing there and the bike went from underneath me.

Oh.

And all of us laughed, and someone ordered another round.

Handful

It's fair to say I might have been a bit of a handful to live with. I lived for football and drinking. And the two often went hand in hand. I'd play football after work for a kickabout, and I'd play a match for Haunchwood at weekends, and there'd like as not be a drink or two involved along the way. But every spare minute I had I'd be playing football. That were my hobby. My life, really.

Of an evening, I'd go up the rec with a bunch of mates and we'd play until it was pitch black. Sometimes, if there was someone with a car, we'd get them to drive the car up and put the lights on, and we'd play by the light of the headlights. Just so we could play for as long as possible. There were no arguments or falling out, just a bunch of lads playing, and it'd be summat like 20-a-side. There were that many of us. On Saturdays, I'd play for Haunchwood, and we were pretty good, if I say so myself. We won the league a couple of times, and got our hands on a few different trophies. One year we won the Chapel End Nursing Cup. It's solid silver and stands about three foot high. It's bigger than the FA Cup, in fact, and worth more, too. Which is why they had to stop playing for it, because insuring it cost too much. It's still in the mayor's office in Nuneaton now, I think...

I were all football. Football, football, football. I played for Haunchwood on Saturdays, another team on Sundays, and if matches got cancelled because of bad weather you might have to catch up on fixtures by having a Saturday League match on a weekday, or a Sunday League match on a weekday. So although I had a couple of girlfriends, football was my life, and there wasn't really much room for a girlfriend. I were all football. I broke my leg playing for Haunchwood once, and when I finally got my leg out of plaster - on a Wednesday - I limped up to watch the match on the Saturday and the coach says *We're short, will you play?*

So I played. Because why wouldn't I? Because everything were football. In an ideal world, I'd like to have been good enough to play for Nuneaton Borough, because they were professional, or semi-professional, but I weren't. So I played for Haunchwood, and I went out drinking. And I came home drunk. And like I say, that might have made me a bit of a handful.

I'd ride home on the Suzuki, drunk. I'd ride it into the garden, down the path, and onto an old door I'd put on the ground for the bike to stand on. Just past this door my dad had sectioned off a piece of the garden, set up a trellis and trained plants up it. It was his pride and joy. And it looked pretty good, till the night I came home a bit more drunk than usual, missed the board, and went straight through the trellis. And no, that didn't help the atmosphere at home. At all.

But then neither did the night I forgot my key. It's two, three o'clock in the morning and I'm hammering on the door and staggering about in the garden. My dad comes to the window. I tell him I've forgot my key.

He says *I know you have. I'll chuck it down to you.*

He throws it down, I miss it in the darkness, and it lands somewhere in the garden. In a bush? On the grass? In the flower bed? I don't rightly know. I'm down on my hands and knees, scrabbling around. I can't find it. So I hammer at the door again, and my dad has to get out of bed to let me in. Next morning, I get up, a bit hungover, and there's a big mound of earth where I'd been scratching around in the darkness trying to find the key, which is lying on the ground next to it, clear as day.

That may have happened more than once, but I only pulled the toilet cistern off the wall the one time. How did it happen? Hard to say. I think I must have been holding onto the pipework while I had a pee, fallen backwards, ripped the whole thing off the wall, thought nothing of it, and gone to bed. The next thing I know, I'm in bed and the old man is shouting me. Water is running down the stairs and out the front door. He's woken up, heard running water, and thought I were having a bath. Then he looks at his bedside clock and thinks *Four o'clock in the morning, and he's having a bath???* And when he got up to see what was happening, there were the cistern lying on the floor, and me spark out in bed, snoring my head off, oblivious.

A lot of these nights out started with me meeting up with my mate Des. Des lived about ten minutes walk from me, and the pair of us would go out drinking and drink really heavy, you know. When the two of us were on a session, we'd start about 6 o'clock in the evening, and finish at 2 o'clock the next morning. We'd down some. And when I say 'some' I mean a lot. This one night I'd been out drinking with Des and at the end of the night when we stumbled back to his he collapsed at the bottom of the stairs. I said to his wife, Carol, *Do you want him upstairs?* She said *Yes please, if you can.*

Bear in mind, I'm drunk as well. I picked Des up, flung him over my shoulder in a fireman's lift, swung him round to carry him upstairs and smashed his head against the wall. We ended up with an ambulance coming, and him in hospital with concussion. Carol was in shock, I think. Her husband had gone from being paralytic to being knocked out.

Next day, when I fetched him out of hospital, he'd got two big black eyes, and he just looked at me and shook his head.

It didn't stop the pair of us going out.

That might well be the same year the two of us went out drinking on Christmas Eve. We got absolutely paralytic, as usual. All I could remember was being really really hungry when I got back home. Next morning, I woke up with this horrible taste in my mouth. What the hell's that? I got up, went downstairs, and my sister says *You'd better get out before my dad comes back.*

Why?

Have a look in the fridge.

I went to the fridge and opened the door. Oh.

See, my dad always used to cook the turkey Christmas Eve, ready for the family coming on Christmas Day afternoon. But I'd come in steaming drunk in the middle of the night, ate the whole turkey, and put the bare bones back in the fridge. That's why my dad wasn't in – he'd gone out to try and find summat else for when the family came round so he wouldn't be asking them to suck on nothing but turkey bones. My sister was right, I had to get out of the way. I went out and stopped out, and didn't darken my dad's door till the day after Boxing Day. He'd calmed down a bit by then.

Another night, I woke up in a ditch. I'd been to a football presentation, and seeing as someone had promised me a lift home, I'd not gone on the bike. But the bloke who was supposed to give me a lift back left early. Or maybe I stayed late. Either way, I ended up walking home. Next morning, I wake up thinking *God, I'm cold!* and realise I'm lying in a ditch. In a couple of inches of water. That was a suit ruined.

A second suit bit the dust after another presentation. I've dressed up for this one. New trousers, new coat, new shirt, new everything. I've had a good night, I've had a bit to drink, and at the end of the night I've decided to walk home. Past Walter's Transport there was a path which went round the back of some garages and brought you out eventually at the back of our garden. Going that way, I'd save a mile and a half walking. More than that by the time I'd gone two forward and three back, which I was. So I go that way. There's a high gate on the path, and I know it's going to be locked, but that's not a problem. I'll just climb over it. That turns out to be a bit more complicated than I'd expected, and in trying to do that, I fall through the gate and get oil all over my new suit. Ah, well.

I finally make it home, get my keys out, and – with

the sort of logic only a very drunk man can manage – I decide the obvious thing to do is smash the window, put my key in the lock from the inside, unlock the door, and let myself in. While I'm at it, I let my dad's Alsatian out, and go to bed leaving all the lights on. Sometime later, my dad wakes up, sees the house lit up like a battleship, comes downstairs, finds the window smashed and the door wide open, and thinks we've been burgled.

He has to go out round the streets to find the dog – because I've let him out but haven't waited for him to come back in again – and it's only when he comes back and sees my clothes lying in a heap, all covered in oil, that the penny drops. He hasn't been burgled. It's his son who's done the damage.

My dad goes mad. He went mad at me a lot, to be honest. He'd be mad at me for trashing the place, and he'd be mad at me for – as he saw it – wasting my money. We must have had this conversation a million times.

Let me save some money for you.
Why?
Well, you might need it some day later on.
What for?
Stuff.
No.
You can't spend it all on beer.
Watch me.
It's silly. Really.
I am silly.

And that were it. Discussion over.

By this time, I were on decent money. My wages had gone up a lot since my first job at Peter Morton's, and now I was on maybe £20-£25 a week, and just paying him board money. Which meant I had a lot to spend on beer. And I didn't mind spending it. And I didn't mind - didn't even notice, if I'm honest - if I were putting my hand in my pocket for drinks and others weren't. And if my dad tried to tell me I was being a mug, well, I wouldn't listen.

How much did you spend last night?
Errrm...
Tell me.
£40.
£40??!!
Yeah.
How many of you was there?
Ten.
Well, somebody ain't paying.
Rubbish.
Ten of you drunk £400 of drink?
Maybe.
Give over!
It's fine.
You've got money, you're paying for them as well.
I ain't.

Now, I look back at it, and he were right. No way we were drinking that much. It was impossible. Beer still weren't that dear. But you're that age, you don't listen, do you? I had money, and what was it for, but to spend? I didn't spend all of it every week, but if it was in my pocket it was burning a hole, so it'd be disappearing soon enough. And if we had a good session, you'd easy spend about thirty, forty quid. Well, I did. I don't know if the others did. I don't know now, and I didn't know then. And I didn't care, either.

My dad was doing what dads do, and trying to tell me to be sensible, but the more dads tell you, the worse you are. Well, I was. When you tell kids *You can't do this! You can't do that!* they'll go and do it behind your back, you know? It was the same for me and my dad.

I was perhaps just a bit more wild than normal.

Quarry

I couldn't fault working for Les. I'd learned mechanics, he'd paid for me to learn to drive, and he'd looked after me. But a couple of years after I'd started there, he cut back on the lorries, and that meant my job went. It were time to find something else. I'd been driving down the quarry for Les, so I thought I'd give working there a go, and I started at the Tilcon quarry in Mancetter, which produced stone for road-building, railway ballast, and the like.

They put me on something they called 'popping'. Once they'd blasted a rockface, they'd feed the stone into a crusher. But however well they blasted a face, there'd be rocks left that were too big - stones needed to be about three foot square to go into the crusher - and that's where my job came in. I'd get up on top of the big rocks with a pneumatic drill, and drill a hole into them. The quarry had three levels, and there were a popper on each level. We'd drill the holes in these rocks, and then the shot firer would come down. He'd fill the holes with explosives, wire them all up, and fire them. If he'd done his job right, it'd smash them to smithereens. If you'd got a big stone and it just broke into four pieces, you might have to pop it again, so smithereens were good.

The foreman over the shot-firers were a little Scotsman, Jimmy. If the shot-firer hadn't turned up, he'd come down and say, in his rough Scottish accent, *He's no here, you can do it yersen.* So we'd load them ourselves. Obviously, when you load them yourself you really want to make sure the rocks blow into small pieces so you don't have to drill them again, so you put a bit extra dynamite in, and then a bit more again, just to be sure. Health & Safety didn't ever come into question.

Did it worry me? No. The way I saw it, this was another string to my bow. And it was fun. I know, to do it properly, you have to have a licence, but that was more for the main blasting. Because when we'd done the popping we used to help the shot-firer anyway, He'd load the holes, and then we'd connect them together with cordex. The only thing we didn't do was load the holes with the dynamite. But if he didn't turn up, the job had got to be done, so you'd get the box and get on with it.

I enjoyed popping. But then they got a machine with a peck on, which would break the stones up, so the shot firing and the popping came to an end. Seeing as I had a driving licence now, I learned to drive a dumper, and spent my working days on that. One by one, I learned how to drive all the machines. Soon enough, it ended up that if someone were off sick or on holiday, I'd just jump on in their place, on whichever machine it was. I loved that. There was always something different to do, and plenty of variation.

The money was all right, too. I was enjoying my work, I had cash in my pocket, and I spent my free time drinking, or playing football. Or drinking after playing football. I'd had a few close scrapes riding the Suzuki after a skinful, and I'd had enough of getting soaked on it when it rained, so when someone else up the quarry offered to swap it for their Mini Clubman, I said yes. It was old, and it was grey, but it kept me out of the weather. And when it fell apart, because I'd got used to having a car, I got myself a second-hand biscuit-coloured Vauxhall Viva instead.

And then the firm my dad was working for went bust, and he needed somewhere to work. So I went and got him a job at the quarry. What else could I do? In the blink of an eye - with all his experience - he'd got himself made up to under-manager. Which was great for him.

But a little bit less good for me.

Lost Licence

You might think, with my dad being under-manager, my job at the quarry would get a little easier. But with him and me not seeing eye to eye, and being all too ready to lock horns, and because I've always been someone to say things as they are, the opposite was true.

The crunch came fairly quickly. There was a bonus scheme in at the quarry and we couldn't ever make the top band. Why? Because the bonus was calculated on the output of four different machines, and in the winter, if it were cold and the belt on the machines had frozen, when you started them up it'd throw the switches and blow the fuses. Muggins here was the bloke with the job of starting the machines up. So if they blew, I had to get the electrician to come out and re-set the fuses. All the guy had to do was press a button when he got there. Open a door, turn the key, job done. It should have been simple. And it would have been simple, if the electrician hadn't lived in Leamington, twenty miles away.

One day the area manager came round to check on things. While he was there, he asked why we weren't making our bonus. So I told him. I explained that when the fuses blew, we had to sit on our hands for an hour while we waited for the electrician to drive over from Leamington. We all knew this made no sense, and we all reckoned there was some kind of sweetener in it for the quarry management, which included my dad. The area manager was furious. He turned round to the old man and the quarry manager and barked *You! And you! Down the office now!*

They got a proper bollocking, and they took it out on me.

In the quarry there was a long belt, maybe forty feet long, which fed the tar plant with aggregate. As the stuff travelled along the belt, some of it would fall off, and - over time - it would pile up underneath the belt. The manager rang me.

You need to go and clean up underneath the belt.
While it's running?
Yes.
Is there anyone to help me?
We ain't got no-one.
OK. No problem.

Cleaning under the belt while it was still running was loud and dangerous. I was on my hands and knees, with the belt running just inches above my head. Nowadays, with Health and Safety, they'd never have got away with making me do it. But things were different then. I cleared all the piles of stone, and rang them back.

I've done that shit job. What do you want me to do now?

That's how things went. They kept piling different things on me, and I just used to do them, turn round and say *Yep, done that. What you got next?* They wanted me to finish, and they thought these jobs would make me quit, but they didn't. I knew what they were doing, and why they were doing it, and I knew I was in the right, too. I've always been the same. If I'm in the wrong, I'll hold my hands up, and say *Sorry, I'm in the wrong.* But if I'm not... nothing will change me.

You can imagine that with all this going on at work, my relationship with my dad was worse than ever. I was determined to spend as little time as possible under the same roof as him, which meant I was out drinking with mates every minute I had. Before too long, the inevitable happened.

I got done for drinking and driving.

I was heading home late one night, and the coppers followed me for three miles. When I got home and parked up, one police car went round the green one way and parked across in front of me, and the other parked across behind me. I got out, and this copper said to me *You were driving in a manner that made us suspicious you've got alcohol in your blood.*

I said *Well why didn't you stop me, then?* but that wasn't going to help. I'd given this copper's brother a good hiding a few months previous, and it was payback time. I were banned for twelve months.

So the car stayed put outside the house, and I got myself a bike and pedalled to the quarry each morning so they could give me shit jobs as a punishment for dobbing them into the area manager.

I started thinking there had to be something better than this.

Marg

And there was. But it wasn't the wrestling. Not yet.

Tilcon had a contract for work in Saudi Arabia. They were laying road and they needed blokes to go out there and work the tar plant. So I put my name down to go. It had to be better than cycling to work in Mancetter in the rain. The Saudi job was for six months. If you passed the interview, Tilcon would fly you out to Saudi, and at the end of each month they'd fly you back for a week at home – if you wanted – and then you'd fly back out for the next month's work. If you didn't want to come back, you could stay there. Either way, the money was out of this world. I wasn't going to miss that opportunity.

I took the interview. I passed. The job was mine. But I wasn't bothered about coming back home once a month. I thought *I may as well stay out in Saudi, I've got nothing to come back for.*

And then fate intervened.

My sister had a mate, Marg. She was married, with four kids, and she lived just down the road. Her husband, Harry, sold insurance and mortgages, and I'd go up the club with him on a Sunday dinnertime and the two of us would have a drink. He was always away at night, supposedly working, so he'd say *Go and sit down with Marg, keep her company, have a cup of tea.* And that's what I did.

The evening I passed the interview, we were having a cup of tea and a chat, and I tells her

I'm going abroad.
What do you mean?
I'm going abroad for work.
No you're not.
Yes I am. It's good money.
No you're not.
I am.
I don't want you to go.

I hadn't expected that.

Next day, I had an accident at work. Somebody left the handbrake off on their lorry, it rolled down the hill, hit my lorry, and trapped me in it. I was really lucky – I wasn't injured, I didn't get so much as a scratch – but it had caved the cab in round me and they had to cut me out to get me free. I came home, and my sister told Marg, and she came up to see me. She knocked the door, and when I opened it the conversation followed on from where we'd left it the night before.

Mac, you're not going to Saudi Arabia.
I am.
You're not, 'cause I'm leaving Harry.

Oh, I thought. And then I kissed her.

I had no idea any of this was going to happen. I knew

I'd begun to have feelings for her, but I hadn't wanted to say anything because I didn't want to mess our friendship up, so I kept them to myself. If I'm honest, it was another reason I wanted to go away to Saudi, so I didn't have to see her. But that evening after the crash, when Marg said she had feelings for me too, and we kissed, well...

That changed everything. I knew right then I wouldn't be going to Saudi.

The two of us sat down and talked, and kissed, and decided we would move in together as soon as I'd found us somewhere to live. Then we kissed some more. And then she went back home. Two hours later, she was back. Harry had threatened her with a knife, and she'd packed her bags and left.

That night, Marg stayed over at my dad's house and I looked in the local paper for somewhere we could live. There was a bedsit for rent. Next day, my dad drove me down in my car to see it. The place wasn't up to much, but we needed something right there and then, so I said *Yes, we'll have it.*

Next day, we moved in.

Bedsit

When I say the bedsit wasn't up to much, I'm not kidding. It was just a bedroom in a house owned by a bloke who lived downstairs and let the three upstairs bedrooms out. We were renting one of them. It was that damp, the wallpaper wouldn't stop on the wall, and they were all covered in mould.

This was my new home. I was twenty years old, I'd moved in with a woman who'd left her husband for me, and of an evening - if it were raining - we could sit and watch the water run down the walls together. For some reason, I wasn't having a drink with Harry up the club on a Sunday anymore. We'd fallen out. He did send his mate round the house with a shotgun, though. I looked at it, looked at him, and said

I do hope that's loaded and you're going to use it. Because if you're not, I'm going to take it off you, shove it up your arse, and blow the top of your head off.

He looked at me, gulped, and said *I'm going.* And he turned round and left. That was the end of that. Why Harry sent him round, I don't know - within days of Marg moving out, he'd had another woman move in with him. Marg swears blind that he'd been seeing her all the time he was supposed to be working late of an evening, that he was being cute when he asked me to go round and keep her company, because of how quick he moved this other woman in. Maybe he was. I don't know. But it brought me and Marg together, so I'm not complaining.

It wasn't an easy time, I'll be honest, but you make the best of it. I was still banned from driving, so I sold the biscuit-coloured Vauxhall Viva and cycled to the quarry every day. Marg got a job at a factory in Mancetter where they made record players, starting out on the soldering, and working her way up to supervisor. We worked, and then we came back home to the bedsit. The kids stayed with their dad. We tried and tried and tried to get them. The solicitor would say *If you can get the kids, we'll get you a property.* And the courts would say *You need a property if you're going to have the kids.* It was Catch 22, and it left us stuck in the bedsit.

We put ourselves on the list for a council house, but that didn't seem to be going anywhere fast. And then Harry dumped two of the kids on us. Tina, the eldest, who was nine or ten; and Neil, the youngest, who was eighteen months old. The four of us, crammed into one room. One damp room. Tina had to sleep on the sofa, and Neil stayed in his carrycot. We lived like that for six months, and all that time the council kept on saying we had to have custody before we could get a council house, and the courts kept on telling us we had to have a house to get custody. And while Harry was happy enough to have us look after the kids, he wouldn't give us custody. It was a no win situation. So in the finish, we had no choice. We had to take the kids back to him.

Living like that wasn't fair on them, and we couldn't do it any more.

Marriage

For all that we were living in a damp, cramped bedsit in a house that had seen better days, and despite the fact Marg was separated from her kids, life was good. We were happy. And in the summer of 1977, once her divorce had come through, I asked her to marry me. And she said yes.

By now, I was working as a driver at Weddingtons Sheet Metal Works. Things at the quarry hadn't got any better, being banned from driving hadn't helped, and I'd had enough of being given the dirtiest, most dangerous jobs. So when I got my licence back after a year and the chance came to make a change, I took it. I left and took a job at Weddingtons as a van driver, doing deliveries. And because I was doing deliveries, they let me take the van home of an evening and park it outside the bedsit.

There was no more cycling to work in the wind and the rain, and I loved it. If things were quiet and I weren't out delivering, I ended up in the workshop, learning how to weld. I learned by watching and doing, like I always did, and before long - from what I'd picked up, what people had showed me - I could gas weld and electric weld, and I was driving out to sites to do whatever welding they needed. One time I was sent over to Hinckley, to one of the hosiery factories there. They'd got this big tank, and it had a hole in one of the seams. I was given the job of welding it.

No problem, I said, and I climbed in the tank. They'd drained it, but the bottom of it was still wet. So as soon as I started welding I was getting a shock. But I done it. This bloke watched me as I worked. And when I finished he said *That's brilliant. Fair play to you, I could see you were getting a shock.* I'm guessing he wasn't the Health and Safety rep. Or maybe he knew I'd a track record of taking on dirty and dangerous jobs. Either way, I hope they dried the tank out properly if they ever needed it welding again. I did quietly suggest that might be an idea...

Anyway, I avoided getting fried, and Marg and myself got married.

We sorted it all out ourselves, paid for everything ourselves, and had a really good time. Marg's dad and her nan came over from Atherstone, and to celebrate the day her nan got her coat cleaned, and we paid for her to have her hair done and bought her a new dress. It was the hottest day of the year, the day we got married, but Marg's nan wouldn't take her coat off, because she'd had it cleaned specially for the occasion. She must have been sweltering, but she kept her coat on all the while, and we might as well not have bothered with her new dress, because nobody saw it.

We got married at a Methodist church in Nuneaton. I'd wanted to get married at Hartshill church, where we'd had my mum's funeral, but the vicar there said he couldn't marry us because Marg had been married before. He said we'd have to get married somewhere else. He thought for a moment and then added *You can come to the church after, and I'll bless you.*

I wasn't having that. I turned round and told him to go away, politely. Well, fairly politely. By which I mean his ears might have burned. I said *If I'm not good enough to be married here I'm not good enough to be blessed.* And I walked off and left Marg standing there. Anyway, we found a Methodist church in Nuneaton that would marry us, and we had the wedding there instead, and it were great.

See, the one thing I won't stand is being treated like muck. I guess I got that from my mum, and I understood why she'd ridden into battle against teachers for me when I was a kid. If someone behaves like the vicar at Hartshill did, I won't take it lying down. It's not in my nature. My temper goes. The same thing had happened in the run up to the wedding, when we went to get our rings. I went in this jewellers with Marg. We'd seen some rings we liked in the window of a jewellers, so in we went. They were serving somebody. So we stood there. As we waited, another couple came in. The jewellers finished serving the first couple and started serving these people. I thought *That's a bit strange.* Then they did it again. And again. Three times they did it, and by now the steam's coming out of my ears. Marg's whispering in my ear *Don't say nothing! Don't say nothing!*

I said *I ain't gonna say nothing.*

Eventually the woman behind the counter got round to serving us. I was definitely going to say something.

Can I help you?

Us?

Yes.

Oh, I thought we was just standing here for ornament.
What do you mean?
You've served three lots in front of us.

I'm sorry, she says - in that tone of voice that tells you she's not sorry at all - *What was you interested in?* I told her we were interested in wedding rings. And I pointed them out. *There's some on this tray, a couple on that tray there, some on that tray in the cabinet, and some on those trays in the window.*

So she gets all these trays out, puts them on the counter, says *Which one would you prefer?* I says *None. You can stick 'em up your arse for making me wait.*

And I walked out.

Fighting

So there you are. Two incidents in quick succession - one with the vicar, the other with the rings - where I left Marg standing while I told someone exactly what I thought of them and stormed out. When I walked out of the jewellers she just stood there gobsmacked, but when she caught up with me she went ballistic. *I knew you were going to do that! I knew you were going to do that! I don't know what you had to do it for!*

I said *I do. It's cos they treated us rotten. It ain't right.*

We went to another jewellers, they sorted us out straight away and we bought the rings there and then. But I've never been one to stand and be messed about. And if I am, I'll say it as it is.

Marg knew what I was, and how I was, and she took me as she found me. Which a lot of people wouldn't do. They'd say I ain't getting into that! The first Christmas I took her out I ended up falling out with somebody at the club. This was Hartshill club, where we had the reception after the wedding, and the guy I fell out with was my best mate's brother, and he were a bit of a... how can I say this...? a bit of a dickhead. He were on the committee and he thought he owned the club. It was about twenty past ten at night, and he picked on me.

Drink your beer! Time to go!
I've got another ten minutes.
No, it's drinking up time!

Yeah, another ten minutes.

No!

The club don't shut till half past...

No!

And then I've got another ten minutes drinking up time.

He wandered off. Then he come round again, ignored everyone else, and started pestering me. Then he poked me. That's a no-no. An absolute no-no. I said

Norman, you'd better go while you can still walk.

You can't hit me, I'm on the committee!

Just go away.

Even his brother told him to leave me alone. And he wouldn't. So I hit him.

He went straight over the top of this little cubicle, flew right over it and was sprawled out along the wall behind it. I said *I did tell him.* I had to go in front of the committee over that. Two or three people come in as witnesses and said *Look, he told him to leave him alone. Why did he just pick on him?* And the committee said if that were the case, just carry on, there's nothing to be sorted out. He stopped pestering me after that, but he'd learned the lesson the hard way.

I never went looking for trouble, but I didn't back down if it came looking for me, either. And it came looking for me quite a bit over the years. There'd always be some bloke - who'd probably had a few pints and thought he was cock of the north - who decided he was ready to have a pop at the big bloke, and who learned too late that it wasn't a good idea.

Back when I was playing football for Haunchwood, a gang of us had gone down to Nuneaton after the game, for a night out. There were a place called the Bondgate Club which had a dance upstairs. We went in, and this guy come over. He wanted to fight me. I just wanted a drink with my mates, so I told him to fuck off.

He kept on and on and on and on and on. In the end I says to him *OK, let's go down into the car park.* I goes down the stairs, with my pint in my hand, and the pair of us squares off in the car park. He takes his coat off, chucks it on the floor. I says to him *Can you just hold my pint for me, while I takes my coat off?* He takes the pint, and as he does I draws my fist back, and hits him. *Bang!*

As he falls back, I takes my pint back out of his hand, says *Thank you very much,* and walks back upstairs leaving him spark out in the car park.

Like I say, it happened a lot. When I was working at the quarry, three lads from Wales come over and I took them out for a drink in Hinckley. We were in the pub, minding our own business, and this guy wanted to arm wrestle me. He'd got a bunch of mates with him, and he kept coming over.

I want to arm wrestle you.
Fuck off, I'm out for a drink with these lads.
I want to arm wrestle you.

He kept on and on. I says to the Welsh lads, *Let's go somewhere else.* I'm driving, and I'm behaving myself, so I'm not drinking. I don't need the aggravation this guy's bringing, but I do need to go to the toilet before we leave. So I nip to the toilet for a piss, and next thing I hear the door bang open. I thought *Here we go...*

I look round and there's six of them lined up. I took a look, picked out the bloke I thought were the biggest one, grabbed him by the throat and the seat of his pants, and rammed his head into the Artex wall as hard as I could. There were blood and snot everywhere, and his mates had lost interest in the prospect of a ruck and were falling over each other trying to get out the door.

He's lying on the floor with blood pouring out of him, and as I'm walking out, the bouncers are coming in. *What's going on in there?*

Oh, I says, *some bloke's tripped up and banged his head on the wall. You need to go and see to him.* We come out, and we're in the car and gone. But everywhere you went, somebody would want to have a crack at you. When I started wrestling, it were even worse. But I were brought up to get the first punch in, and that stood me in good stead.

Marg did her best to be a civilising influence, but it was an uphill struggle, and it didn't always work. One year, Haunchwood had won the Chapel End Nursing Cup, which was a big deal - and a big cup - round our way. It's solid silver, stands three foot high, and is bigger than the FA Cup. It's worth more, too, which is why they had to stop playing for it, because insuring it cost too much, and why it's now sitting in the mayor's office in Nuneaton.

Anyway, this year Haunchwood had won it. We'd had a few drinks up the club to celebrate, and I'd come home to get changed for a special event that night. Marg is coming along too, and as we get ready she says to me

I know you're going to have more drinks...
I am.
But don't start fighting.
No, I won't.
Promise me you won't start.
I promise you I won't start.

We're at the club, filling the Chapel End Cup with beer and taking it round to everyone to have a drink. This guy has had his, but he keeps coming back, wanting some more, and I keep shoving him away, telling him *No, wait till the end. If there's some left when everyone's had their drink, you can have it all.* He kept coming back, I kept saying *No, you're not having any more!* and he decides he's going to fall out with me. He goes home, comes back in his work clothes, and says *I want you outside.*

Marg looks at me and says *You promised!* And she's right, I had. No fighting. No problem.

I go outside, and tell him straight *I don't want to fight you* - I did really, of course - *I don't want to fight you. I'm having a good time, so please just leave me alone.* As I turn round to walk away he hits me in the side of the face and splits my lip. That's it. He's asking for it. I'm going to hit him. And then I tell myself *No! I promised Marg I wouldn't.* So I grab him by the arse and the throat, and chuck him straight over the top of his car. He hits the wall the other side, and that's the end of that.

I walk back in to Marg and tell her *I didn't fight. But don't ever ask me not to.* And I showed her my lip, with a big blood blister on the inside. *That's what I got because I didn't hit him first.* See, I was taught, always get the first one in. Nine times out of ten that put them away, and if it didn't, they weren't in no condition to give me the second one. That's how I were brought up, and it worked, especially when you'd got these idiots coming up and wanting to fight.

I knew I could handle myself, but I got fed up with having to. I just wanted to go out with my mates, have a quiet drink, have a good time, and enjoy myself. But no. Sometimes going out meant I had to throw someone over a car, or get them to hold my pint while I hit them, or introduce them to an Artex wall they needed to get up close and personal with, and Marg knew that. She understood it. And she were great. She backed me in everything I done.

Council House

Marg and me lived in the bedsit, with the water running down the walls, for a year or two. I was working at the quarry to start with, and then the sheet metal works, and Marg had a job at a factory in Mancetter where they made record players. She worked her way up and became supervisor. We'd come back from work and stay in of an evening, and Marg was always busy knitting.

One night I says to her, *I can knit.* She says, *Yeah, I'll bet you can.* Now, my mum had taught me, years before. So I says *Give me a pair of pins and some wool...* and I showed her. She were quite shocked.

Over a few weeks, I knitted a jumper. A plain jumper. Marg was doing cable, and I fancied learning that. She kept showing me how to do it, I'd have a go, but I kept getting it wrong. Then I'd pass it to her to undo, and she'd put me right. In the finish, she must have got bored with me.

Right, she says, *you want to learn cable?*

Yeah.

If you go wrong, you undo it yourself.

And that's what I did.

That's how I learned how to do cable. Being me, I weren't satisfied with that. I started knitting with different colours, and then I knitted a cardigan for my nephew. He were mad about Wolves, he were all Wolves, and I decided to knit him a top. A zip-up cardigan, and it would be really, really special. I got one of my old *Football Monthly* magazines, traced the picture of a player kicking a ball, and copied it onto a piece of draught paper. Every little square was a stitch. I coloured it in, and Marg and me sat and counted the squares and worked out the pattern. Then I knitted it. It looked absolutely brilliant. It had a footballer on the back, and WOLVES on the front. WOL on one side of the zip, VES on the other. My nephew absolutely loved it. He wore that cardigan for years.

Knitting. That might not be what you expect a big old lump of a wrestler to do. But why not? It were me learning by doing, again, just the way I'd learn how to do wrestling when the time came. And it were me being interested in learning something new, and working with my hands, and being happy to do so.

We had it rough in that bedsit, though. We kept trying to get a council house, but we hadn't got the points. Marg was going through her divorce, but without a place we couldn't get custody of her kids, and without the kids, we couldn't get a place. Then the guy downstairs moved out.

Who should we pay the rent to now? We didn't know. Marg told her solicitor and he said *That's OK, don't pay anything, you're a squatter now.* She panicked, because squatters meant bailiffs, squatters weren't respectable, but I said, *Hold on. He's told us not to pay anything, so we don't pay anything.* And we didn't.

I don't know how he did it, but within a couple of weeks the solicitor had got us a council house. Marg and me finally had our first proper house together, on

Whittleford Road, Stockingford. It was a big improvement on a place where the wallpaper didn't stay on the walls, believe me, but we had a laugh in that bedsit. We had some good times. And I learned to knit cable.

Life's what you make it, ain't it?

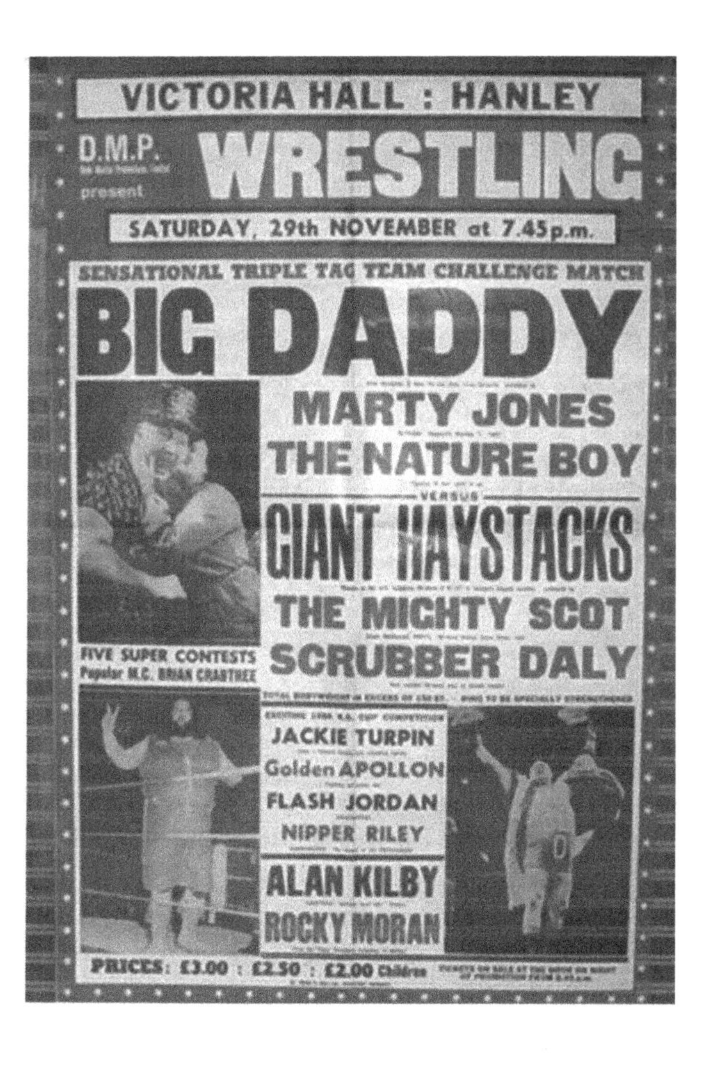

my future was on its way...

Phone Call

Meeting Marg, marrying her, and moving into the council house had a huge impact on my life. It was lots of change, and all for the good. There were setbacks, yes, but we took them in our stride. I was working at the sheet metal place, and when Marg lost her job at the record player factory because it closed down, these were still the days when you could walk out of one job and into another. One day we were walking through Nuneaton and I lost her. The Co-op were opening a new 'budget bar' shoe shop and we walked past and she popped in and asked if there were any jobs going. They had. She started there and then.

We were working. We were doing up the council house. Our treat to ourselves was going to the wrestling at Bedworth each month, watching people like Marty Jones, Mal Kirk, Pat Roach, Rollerball Rocco and the like ply their craft, with us sat in the front row just a few feet away from them. I loved it. I enjoyed the spectacle of it like nothing else I knew, and it reminded me how my grandad and grandma would have wrestling on the telly on a Saturday afternoon, how my mum watched *World of Sport* too, how me and her would go along to the wrestling when we were on holiday in Weymouth each year, and how she loved Johnny Kwango.

It never entered my head to think *I'll have a go at that!* I just enjoyed having a night out, sitting with Marg and a beer, and watching wrestlers I'd seen on the TV, so close

I could hear them, so close I could see the sweat and the effort.

Then, early in 1983, the sheet metal company went bust. Suddenly getting another job wasn't quite as easy. To bring some money in, I'd do bits and pieces for my mate - window cleaning and that - and he'd slip me a few quid, and out of that we'd pay all the bills and save a bit for the wrestling, because that was all we had, really.

And then, don't ask me why, but at the end of one of the wrestling nights at Bedworth I picked up one of the programmes and wrote to Dale Martins.

I'd like to become a wrestler. How do I do that?

I hadn't told Marg I was doing this, so when Dale Martins got back to me to say that Pat Roach was doing a wrestling course in Birmingham - and gave me his phone number - I was over the moon, but at the same time I knew I had to tell Marg. What if she thought this was a daft idea? What if she thought I was wasting my time?

I needn't have worried. Marg were great. She listened, and said

Well, if that's what you want to do... Do it.

Proof, once more, that I'd married the right woman.

I picked up the phone, and I rang Pat Roach.

That one small act would change my life in ways I couldn't imagine.

Pat Roach

The good news was that here I was, chatting on the phone to a real-life wrestler, someone I'd sat and watched from the audience in Bedworth. The bad news was that straight away, I ran into a problem. I asked Pat about the wrestling course, and he told me it lasted eight weeks. And it cost £150.

I hadn't got £150. Marg and me were getting by from week to week, covering the bills. There wasn't £150 squirrelled away under a mattress anywhere, and I couldn't see how that was going to change. We hadn't got the money, and I couldn't do the course. Realising this took everything out of me, and I sunk.

Then one day I was at my mate's, cleaning the windows, doing the gardening, and he said *What's up with you?* So I told him. *Don't worry about it,* he said, *I'll sort that.* Fat chance, I thought. But to my surprise, he did. He got ten of his mates together and they each put about £20 a piece in. That was enough to pay for the training, and for me to buy the leotard and the boots as well. And that were the beginning, that were how things started, through the generosity of a mate and his friends.

I rang Pat and told him mates of mine had put the money together, and he said that was fine, and then I asked him if he could come over so the local paper could take a photo, and he said *Of course I can.* And he did. The paper was the *Nuneaton Evening Tribune,* who did two or three write-ups on me when I started. There was one photo where Marg's got me in a headlock, one where Pat came over, and another one, when I hurt my neck at Ashton-under-Lyme, but that was later on. Let's not get ahead of ourselves. I'd got the money, and I rang Pat, and we arranged for him to come over to Nuneaton and get his photo took with me and the ten people and the cheque. That way, everybody got a bit of publicity.

When Pat came over, it was the first time I'd properly met him. I'd seen him on TV, of course, and I'd seen him wrestle at Bedworth. I'd even chatted to him on the phone. But what would he really be like? The good news was that Pat was an ordinary guy. No airs and graces. If you'd seen him in the street, you would never have known he were famous - even though by then he'd been in the *Conan* films, he'd been in *James Bond*, so he were pretty well known. But he came over as an ordinary guy. He shook hands with everyone and chatted away. This is a first, he said, having a bunch of people club together for someone to learn to wrestle.

He told everyone there, to their faces *Look, I can teach him how to wrestle, but he might get in there the first time, get smacked in the nose, and say no this ain't for me. So I don't want any comebacks on me.*

And everyone nodded and said *Yep, that's fine. But if he gets a smack in the nose he'll probably end up giving one back.* Because they knew me and what I was like! Pat laughed at that, shook hands with everyone again, put the cheque in his pocket, and left.

That was August or September, 1983. A month or so later, I was standing at Nuneaton station with my boots and my leotard in a bag, heading for Birmingham to start training with Pat Roach.

I was going to be a wrestler. I knew it.

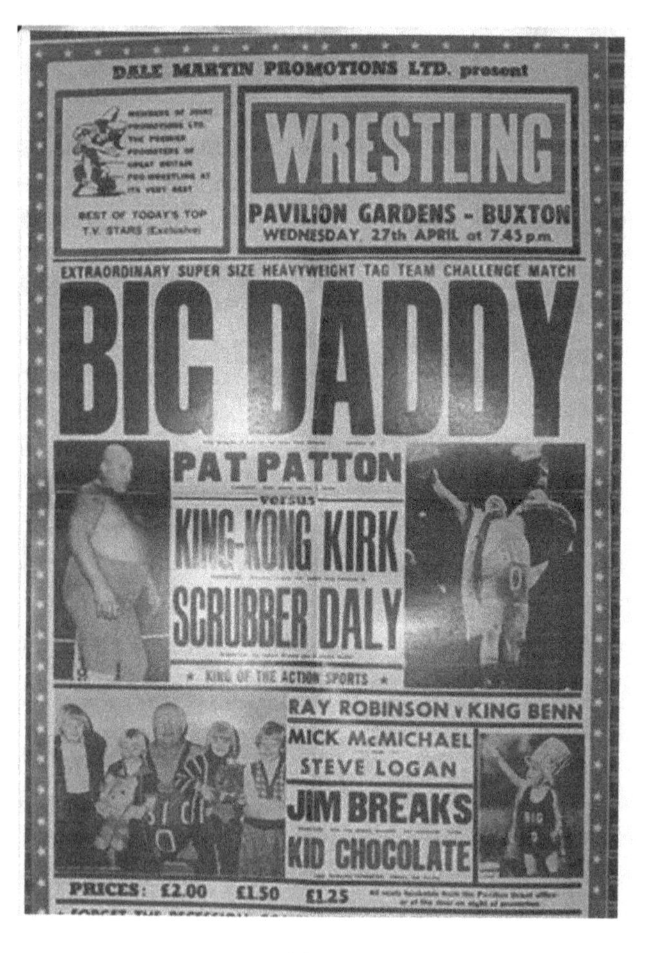

told you...

Training

Pat had got a gym in the centre of Birmingham, just above Woolworths, right by the Bullring. There was no parking there, and I didn't fancy driving anyway, so it were easier, and cheaper, to get the train.

I was nervous. I was excited. I was wary about what was going to happen. Pat never give anything away when he came over and met us, just said *I can teach him, but...*

So that first Saturday morning when I walked out of New Street station in Birmingham on the way to start my training, I didn't know what to expect. I knew I had to be outside Woolworths at nine in the morning each day, and we'd be there till six. It was going to be a long old day, but I didn't mind that. Then I turned the corner and saw a queue of people there. All of them waiting to start the course, same as me.

There were 136 of us. At £150 a pop.

We go in, we get changed. Pat comes in, says a few words, we get to it. That first session, Pat gets us all to link up referee's hold, where you come together and clasp. Then he teaches us the bumps. From there, he takes us into a headlock, a wrist lock, simple things like that. He weren't there all the while, either. The way the day worked was that Pat would come in, have a chat with you, get you doing moves, and then he'd leave you to carry on doing the moves but move around doing them with different people. That way you worked with different people all the while. Then he'd come back, have another chat, say *We'll do so-and-so to lead into this...* bit like we do with the training now, to build up to a whole match.

I tell you now, nine in the morning till six of the evening is a long time to be thrown around on concrete, because that's what happened. There were no mats in Pat's gym, just carpet on a concrete floor, and sometimes Pat would walk in, pick someone up, and slam them on the floor. Mainly, that person was me, that's what it felt like. I was the biggest one there, and I swear now he only slammed me into the floor so often to see if I'd keep going. To test me. Nowadays, wrestlers have it easy. We'll be training, and Matt'll say *Get a couple of crash mats!* More often than not he'll hear me mutter *Why you got to get them?* And he looks at them and smiles, because he knows what I mean. We never had crash mats, it was just a concrete floor with a carpet on.

The first time Pat picked me up and slammed me into the floor was the afternoon of that first training session. We'd started at nine, we'd had half an hour break for lunchtime - and there were people who didn't come back after lunchtime that first day, which gives you an idea of how hard it could be - and then in the afternoon, Pat just walked in, picked me up, and slammed me on the floor. He didn't say what he was going to do. Just SLAM! Pure strength. He'd shown us the bumps that morning, shown us roughly how to fall, but he'd thrown us when he was stooping down and you'd take the back bump. Now a six-foot guy was lifting me up in the air...

I must admit I thought *I'm going to die here!!* He picked me up, and *Boom!* down I went.

At the time, I weighed about 21 stone. So Pat was making a point, picking me up. Whatever the point was. That he could, probably. I don't think it was any more complicated than that. What did I feel when he did it the first time? *Fuck this! I ain't doing this no more!* But, obviously, I did. Why? Because I loved it.

That might sound mad. It might be a bit mad, I don't know. The first time Pat slammed me, I hit that concrete floor and thought *Oh my god, what the hell am I doing here??*

Then the adrenalin kicked in, and I thought *I haven't broke nothing, I'm still moving... and if I can do that here, on a concrete floor, it's going to be a lot easier when I do it in the ring, because the ring's got a bit of spring in it.* And I got back up to my feet, and I carried on.

That was how wrestling was back then. Nigel Hanmore learned his wrestling at the London gym, where Mike Merino would stack chairs 5-6 foot high, put a mat down, and tell the trainee wrestlers to jump off the chairs and land flat on their front. As they jumped, he'd pull the mat away, and they'd land on the concrete floor.

It was mainly to see if you'd come back, to sort out the ones who really wanted to learn to wrestle from the ones who didn't. And it worked. There were 136 of us at Pat's gym that first morning. I'd say about 20-odd packed their bags and went on the first day, just sloped off and never came back. As the course went along, more and more and more people dropped out.

There was one guy that Pat was suspicious of, who came along to the sessions in a mask. He came in on the same bus as one of the other lads, and he said the guy was wearing a mask on the bus, too. After a couple of weeks, Pat pulled me to one side and said *I'm a bit wary about the guy with the mask.* I asked why.

Pat said *He could be from a newspaper. Do you think you could rip the mask off him?* I says *If that's what you want, yes, I can do that.* So Pat shows us a move, puts us in pairs, and puts me with the masked man. I was throwing him around a bit and he were getting a bit agitated. I thought *Now's the moment!* And I ripped his mask off. He turned round and left and we never saw him again.

Pat took me on one side again – that were one thing with Pat, if he wanted to tell you something, he'd take you on one side – and said *Thank you. I'm not 100% sure if he was a reporter, but he hasn't come back, so I think he could have been.*

There was nothing for him to report anyway. It was just a bunch of blokes paying money to be thrown around on concrete by a bloke who'd been in the movies and who turned up each week to a gym in the centre of Birmingham with his stuff in a plastic carrier bag. A man who had no airs and graces, who'd have forgotten some of his kit nine times out of ten and need to borrow your towel or your trunks, who never ever rubbed his fame in your face. Pat was a top wrestler, and he absolutely looked the part. More than that, he was a fantastic bloke.

One hundred and thirty-six men started that wrestling course. Three of us finished.

It was Scott Conway, Andy Blair, and me. I'd learned a lot, but right up until I had my first match, I didn't know nothing. Only that we were wrestlers now, and we were going to knock seven bells out of each other, given the opportunity.

Brent

After about five weeks' training with Pat, numbers had just dwindled away and dwindled away. There were about a dozen of us left by then, and Pat took us over to Digbeth Town Hall to meet Max Crabtree, who was up there for a wrestling event. For Pat to take us along to meet Max, he must have felt there was a decent chance we'd all carry on and take up wrestling, but as I said, in the end just three of us did.

The meeting with Max was like having an interview - you knew a lot depended on how this went, because Max ran a lot of the wrestling in the UK. His job was to put on shows, fill the venues, and make as much money as he could.

I went in to see him and he said *Grow a beard, you're too baby-faced to be a villain. And put some weight on.* I was 21 stone then. I thought I was big enough. But Max wanted me for Big Daddy.

In the weeks after that meeting, I kept writing to him, asking when he was going to get me in. Every week I sent a letter, because Pat had said *Keep pestering Max, keep pestering him.* So I did.

Was it a test? Oh yes. Everything was. It must have been about six weeks after that interview at Digbeth that I got my first match, and I'd written to him six times in those six weeks.

When Max gave me my first match, that was in Brent, and that was another test.

My first ever wrestling match was me versus Andy Blair. He drove down from Cannock and parked his car at the Novotel in Bedworth, I met him there, and we travelled down to Brent Town Hall together. Driving down was nerve-wracking. Really nerve-wracking. My stomach were turning over, and I must have stopped three or four times for a wee. This was going to be the first time either of us had wrestled in the ring or in front of a crowd.

The only time I'd been in a ring at all before that was when we met Max in Digbeth, when all of us had walked across Birmingham from Pat's in our normal clothes, and got in the ring that was set up for that night's show at the Town Hall, just so we could see what it was like. That was the only time a lot of them ever got in the ring – there, in Digbeth Town Hall, in their ordinary clothes, as part of our day of meeting Max Crabtree.

This match at Brent would be the second time either Andy or I had got in the ring. We badly wanted to get everything right. We had to be there for half past six for a half past seven start, and we got there early, because we didn't want to get caught out by London traffic and be late on our first day. We drove down, we parked up, and we went in separately.

Why? Because Pat had told us *If you're wrestling each other, don't go in together, don't walk in together – you don't want people waiting outside to see you walking in together and being matey.*

It makes sense. If you're going to get in the ring and make out you hate each other, and want people to believe it, you can't stroll in laughing and joking, can you? Later, when I was wrestling as the Masked Marauder, I've even had to get out the car 2-3 minutes away and walk down the street with a bonnet on so no-one knows who it is. You imagine doing that now - walking down the street with a mask on, you'd have coppers all over you. But it was the way things were then. And it kept the punters wondering all the while, you know, and they couldn't say *Those two have travelled down together, what's that mean?*

Anyway, Brent. We got down there, walked into the dressing rooms, and nobody spoke to us. Not a word. Back then, when you turned up as a new wrestler, the regular guys looked at you as someone who could potentially be taking their spot in the future. And given the way Max Crabtree worked, they had good reason. So we sat in the corner, tried not to show we were nervous, and waited.

Who was on the bill that night? I think there was Sid Cooper, Steve Grey, Tom Tyrone and Pete Roberts, and a few more... two London lads, I would imagine. I think the Bear Man were on, Johnny Elijah, and The Emperor, who was in a mask. And none of them spoke to us.

Andy and I went on second, just before the interval, kicked the crap out of each other, come off, and suddenly all of the wrestlers were laughing and chatting with us, because they'd all been watching our match. Everyone watches a wrestler's first match to see what you know and what you do, and whether you're up to it.

I think we must have passed the test. And now I was buzzing. There'd been a lot to take in. My first proper bout. My first time wrestling in a ring. My first time in front of a crowd - and there were maybe 200 people in there, which is a good crowd, and they were loud. Very loud. My first time meeting other wrestlers.

It was an eye-opener as regards the actual job.

I was a heel then, and when a heel goes into the ring, and the crowd all boo you, you get a buzz, the adrenalin starts running. The crowd booing me, it lifted me. And the more I did, the worse they got, the more they booed. I couldn't tell you what Andy and I did in the ring, but I can tell you it were good. We got them really worked up, so considering it was the first time for everything, it were good. While we were in the ring, I were concentrating on what I was going to do, what Andy was doing, what would happen next, how to fall. The high, the oh-my-god-I-love-this only came after, when we got back to the dressing room and sat down and the other wrestlers started talking to us.

When we were in the ring we could see them watching. Tom Tyrone, Pete Roberts, the Bear Man, they were all in my bracket, heavyweights, and I could have gone on with them. The others, Sid, Stevie Grey, could all work with Andy. So Tom and Pete were chatting with me and giving me advice, and Sid and Stevie were chatting to Andy.

Coming back from Brent we were on such a high it was like we were floating up the motorway. And when I got home I was awake for about four hours, still buzzing. I'd got the day off work the next day, so that was all right, but at some point during that day I started stiffening up, noticing the bumps and the bruises. Definitely. But driving back after a match - especially your first match - you're on such a high you don't feel them. And you'll get them every time.

Brent was a great night. Then, it was a matter of waiting. About a month later, I got a date sheet come through, with four dates on it. For the whole month. That's how it worked. At the end of the month you'd get a date sheet for the next month, and you had to let them know which ones you could do. The first one I had was up north somewhere, and I'd got to meet Pat Patton at Junction 12, by the transport cafe, the greasy spoon. I parked my car there, met Pat, and we headed north up the M6. I can't remember where we were going, but I know it was with Pat.

Later in my career, by the time I was working five or six days a week, I wasn't noticing the bumps and the bruises any more. I got used to them. But that first night after Brent, me and Andy were rattling away as we drove back up the motorway. It seemed like we were in the car five minutes and I were back at Bedworth, dropping him off. It were absolutely brilliant.

I thought *Yeah, I'm going to make a go of this. If I get the chance, this is for me.*

Date Sheets

That match at Brent was the first time we'd been in the ring, in front of the crowd. And now we watched and learned. Because the other wrestlers knew the ropes, pardon the pun. They knew how to use the ring in a way we were only beginning to work out. Andy and me stayed, and watched, and learned by watching. I still watch all the matches at an event, even now. I always sit and watch as many as I can. Now it's mainly so I can tell Matt what's wrong and what's right - but back then, the more you watched, the more you picked up, and then you'd use it in your own way. And then the other lads would help you as well. Mal Kirk, he helped me a lot. Stacks did, too. You were learning all the while, and you never stop learning really. Pat Patton, who I did my next match with, he helped me a hell of a lot. We become real good friends. Him and his wife, me and Marg. But for now, that's all in the future.

As I say, I had to wait about a month after Brent for my date sheet. And when it came, it had four dates on it. Which was fairly standard, really. Part of how Max worked was to make sure you knew that you needed him more than he needed you. That you didn't think you had the upper hand, or could ask for anything more than he was ready to give you. He'd have shows on every night of the week, all over the country - he might have four or five shows a night - but he'd a lot of wrestlers on the books, all of them after the work. So you took what you were given, and I'd been given four dates.

I done three of those four dates, and then Johnny England got the sack. Max sacked him. Next day I got a full date sheet for the month. I'd started with four, done three, and then I'd got a full month, because they'd given me all his jobs.

Johnny had got sacked because he'd been wrestling for All-Star Promotions. and back in those days you either worked for Max, or for All-Star. You couldn't work for both. And he'd done jobs for them, and Max had found out, so he sacked him. And I got all his jobs. That was the turning point for me – things just flew from there. The first one of his jobs I did was in Girvan, in Scotland. I'd got a job at the quarry again by now, so I'd been to work for the day, finished work, gone home, washed, changed, and met Pat Patton at Cannock, and then he drove up to Girvan, which is a fair old slap.

This is still very early days for me and wrestling. I knew I loved it, but I didn't yet know how it worked, especially when it came to money. For Brent I'd got a fiver, and I didn't even know to ask for petrol money. Pat did, of course. When we got back from Girvan, Pat stopped the car, turned to me and said

Have you got your petrol money?
What petrol money?
You're supposed to get petrol money.
I am?
And you give it to me because I drove.
I do?

So I showed him my pay packet – that way he could see I was telling the truth. Next day he must have rung Max and had a word, because from then on I got the petrol money each time. Pat was driving, so I'd get to keep the 'meet money' which was from home to where we met, and then Pat got the rest.

The way it worked, if there were four of you in the car, the driver got paid for three, if there were two or three in the car, whoever was driving got paid for two. So that weren't bad. You could make your money up by being the driver, but most of the time I was happy for Pat or someone else to drive, while I relaxed. When you've been at work all day, like I had, you didn't really want to drive up to Scotland and back and then go to work the next day. OK, it might make you £40, and petrol weren't very dear, so you could make some good money at it – more than you'd make from being in the ring – but even so, I wasn't interested. I think some wrestlers saw themselves as drivers who did a bit of wrestling on the side. In fairness, I think all of us did at one time or another!

Those hours spent travelling up and down the motorway to shows were just as much part of the job as the minutes in the ring. They were good fun. If there were three or four of you in the car you'd have a laugh and a joke, and the miles flew by and it were great.

In all my years of wrestling, the only exception I can think of, the only time I had a real bad trip was when I wrestled in Leeds one Thursday. I stopped at the promoter's house in Leeds that night, and the next day I were going up to Edinburgh with Kwik Kick Lee, who couldn't speak english, and Alan Kilby, who were deaf and dumb. So I travelled all the way up there and back, and never said a word. Him in the back of the car couldn't speak english, and Kilby couldn't speak.

If you think Alan's deafness was just a gimmick by the way, you'd be wrong. He really was deaf and dumb. At first I didn't like wrestling him because when you hurt him, he didn't squeal, and that made it less of a spectacle. That's hard work for a heel like me. Normally when the blue eyes squeal, the crowd hate you even more than they did before. You didn't get that with Alan. What you did get was that the crowd felt sorry for him. That was good, and Alan knew to play up to it - the poor deaf and dumb bloke being bullied by a nasty man. He always had a bloke in the corner, and Alan would sign to him - the bloke hadn't a clue what he was saying, but Alan would sign - and the crowd would feel even sorrier for him.

What that meant was the more you done to him, the more heat you got. I enjoyed working with him, actually. He just wasn't great conversation in the car.

At this point, I've been wrestling for two months. I've made my debut in Brent, got my first date sheet, done three jobs out of the four - all with Pat Patton - and then I've inherited Johnny Englands' date sheet and my feet haven't touched the ground.

I'm on my way. Happy days.

Rise

By the time I finished that first date sheet, I'd been a professional wrestler for eight weeks. How different a wrestler was I at the end of that time, compared with when I got in the ring at Brent? Oooh. I'd say 100% different. I'd learned how to use the ring and the ropes to my advantage, I'd learned more of the technical stuff I needed to know, I'd learned some of the ways I could best upset a crowd. All that kind of thing. I was a lot lot better, but I still weren't finished. Nowhere near. My Uncle Brian used to say to me *You're never too old to learn.* He was right - and this was a real learning curve - but that weren't the half of it.

By the end of that month when I took on Johnny English's dates, I was shattered. I didn't know if I were coming or going. I was wrestling each evening. I was working all day. And on top of that, at the weekends, I was doing a milk round, too.

Why was I doing a milk round? Well, while I'd been out of work, I picked up a job doing a Friday night, Saturday morning, and Sunday milk round for these two ladies. They gave me the work to help me out. At the same time I was doing a little bit of window cleaning for Bill - that's the guy who organised his mates to chip in to pay for my training - too. Then I'd got the job at the quarry, and now I was wrestling as well, and it was the summer shows, so wrestlers were out every night. The upshot of this was that I was working at the quarry seven days a week, seven nights a week I was wrestling, and then Saturday and Sunday I was crawling out of bed - if I'd even got into it - to do the milk round.

I was like a zombie.

Marg was worried. She knew this wasn't sustainable. She also knew how stubborn I was. The job at the quarry was my bread and butter, and there was no way on earth I'd stop wrestling, so she had a word with the two ladies. She told me the boss, Vicky, wanted a word with me.

My first thought was that I'd done something wrong, that I'd been so tired I'd missed getting a payment off someone and the money were short. She told me it was nothing like that. Vicky told me straight.

Look, Mac, we don't want no arguments -
Me neither.
- but you've got to stop doing the milk.
Why?
Well...
What have I done?
You're going to kill yourself.
I'll be fine...
It's just too much.
But...
We're not letting you do it, and that's it.

And it was. I really appreciated what they'd done for me at a time when I needed it, because it kept me going. We parted good friends, and that was that.

Now I was just - just! - working seven days a week at the quarry, and wrestling seven nights a week. Easy. And because I was only on a temporary contract at the quarry, I'd got an arrangement where I could finish a shift early if I needed to. If I were wrestling in Scotland, say, I could leave at midday so I could get there in time. The downside was this meant I'd be starting work at four in the morning so I'd completed my shift by dinnertime. It worked out - kind of - and I could keep both the work and the wrestling going, but even after being sacked from the milk round for my own good I was completely and utterly knackered.

The hours I was doing were ridiculous, but - honestly, hand on heart - there wasn't ever a time when I thought about getting in the wrestling ring and dreaded it, or when I turned in a shoddy performance. Because once I got in there, and the crowd started shouting and bawling, I got the buzz, and I were off. Every time. It livened me up, like. Even though I was exhausted sometimes, I'd get in the ring and be away again.

I knew I just had to get through the summer. When the summer season finished, things got a little quieter, and I'd be out maybe four or five nights a week. That wouldn't be so bad. The summer season ran from June through to the end of August, and then you'd be out seven nights a week, up and down the country. We'd be doing the seaside places: Skegness, Brighton, Southport, Blackpool, Great Yarmouth, Bournemouth, Morecambe, Barry Island, Rhyl, Llandudno. (Those last two were for Oreg Williams. Max would let you work for him, for some reason.)

That summer, every single day without fail, I got in the ring no matter what. I never missed a show, I never grumbled. Don't get me wrong, there'd be days where I'd think *God, I've got to get up to Leeds, or Colne, or wherever, and I really can't be bothered...* But once you got on the road that were it. Especially if you'd picked somebody else up, or once you met up with somebody, you'd just have a laugh in the car all the way up there and all the way back. The worst bit of the whole night was when you got back to your own car and you went your separate ways and you'd got to drive home those last few miles.

Trying to keep awake when you were dead on your feet. That was the worst. How we weren't killed, all of us, I don't know. I was talking to Pete Lapaque the other day, and he said it's unbelievable - when you look back at it - unbelievable that none of us died. We were exhausted. You'd be driving up the motorway and there'd be nothing in front of you, and then you'd blink, and suddenly there'd be a lorry there. You'd nodded off. Just for a moment, perhaps, but a moment's long enough to veer into another lane or onto the hard shoulder - no rumble strips back then - and then you're in a world of trouble.

That's why, if I were travelling on my own, Marg would always come with me. It was someone to talk to, someone to make sure I didn't nod off at the wheel, someone to share the driving if I really couldn't keep my eyes open.

I remember once, coming back from Blackpool. Marg was still learning to drive - I was teaching her the basics and then she'd have a few proper lessons to polish things off, that was the plan. Anyway, we're coming back from

Blackpool, and I were absolutely shattered. So we pulled in the services, I took the L plates off the car, and told her

You're driving the rest of the way home.
I can't do that!
You can.
I can't!
You can.
You'll be asleep!
I will.
But...
Just get in the slow lane...
I can't!
Keep it at 60...
Mac...
And nobody will bother you.

And that's what she did. And it was fine. She did that a few times, to be fair. Another time we were coming back from Blackpool and I'm asleep in the passenger seat, and suddenly Marg's shaking me. *Mac! Mac! Mac! There's blue lights! What am I going to do??* I said just keep going, as you are, it'll be fine. By the time we got to the blue lights, they were on the other side of the motorway!

I said *You woke me up for nothing now!*

That didn't go down too well. It didn't go down well at all.

there's a lot of fun to be had...

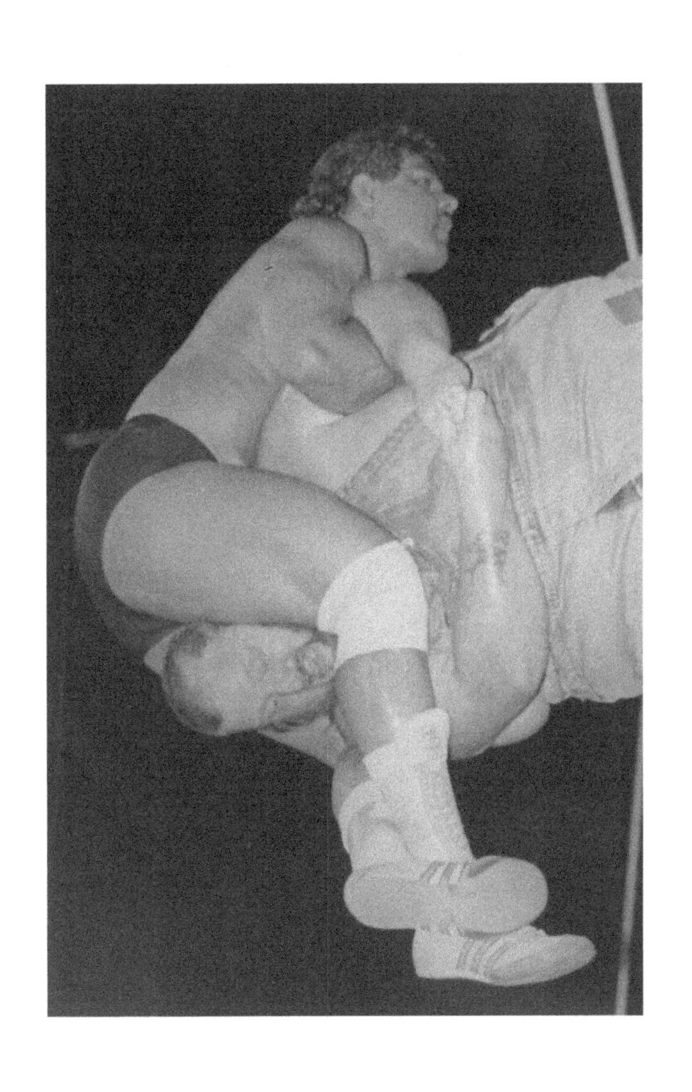

when you're a heel

Team Scrubber

The one thing I could always count on was that Marg had got my back. She always had done, right from the start. Whatever I've done: football, cricket, wrestling, she always backed me. And if anybody took the mickey because I were big, she'd rip their throat out.

Back when I was playing football for Haunchwood, she was working in Nuneaton, in the offices of a place that made machine tools. A bloke comes in, starts chatting.

We played Haunchwood last week.
Did you?
Yes, they've got this big fat goalkeeper...
Really?
I was taking the mickey out of him.
Oh yeah?
Yeah.
That's my husband.

And she looked at him.

Errr...
It's no problem...
I meant...
But he will be here in half an hour to pick me up.
Oh.
If you want to say anything to him...

No.
You sure?
I've gotta go, I've gotta go.

And he shot off. Well, about a month later, we were playing this team again. He came into the offices, so Marg took the chance to wind him up.

You know he's got your name in his book, don't ya?
Who?
My husband.
What d'ya mean?
When you take the mickey out of him...
Yeah?
He's got a little book. He puts people's names down.
He doesn't!
He does, I assure you.
Oh god.
He'll get his own back, you mark my words.

And the bloke would not play in that game. He cried off. He wouldn't play.

Marg always had my back, and I always had hers. That was how it was. After we moved out of the bedsit and into our first council house, there was a knock on the door one night - I used to play six-a-side football on a Monday night but this night it had been cancelled and I was at home - and Marg went to the door and it was her two eldest, Colin and Tina. We'd been trying and trying to get custody of her four kids, but without any success, and now here were two of them, on the doorstep. Tina was thirteen. Colin was about twelve. They said *Dad's dropped us off, he don't want us no more.* And all they had with them was a little shoebox each.

Marg was so happy to see them, but when she asked them to come in, Colin wouldn't. He told us

My dad says Mac'll get drunk and beat us up.

He'd been away with his dad for six months or so, and this was what he'd been told. How do you deal with that? We did the only thing we could - we left the front door and the back door open for him so he knew he could get out anytime he wanted. It took him about three months to feel safe, but it was never a question that we'd do anything else. We used to make him and Tina write to their dad every week, but he never replied, ever. Eventually they decided they weren't going to write to him any more. It was a rough time, but we stuck together and looked after each other.

It's what you do, isn't it? Like when Marg and me first got together, she'd go over to Atherstone where her dad and gran lived together, and do the washing for them and bring it back and I'd iron it, and do odd jobs for them at weekends. They were lovely, her dad and gran. When her gran had a tumble and broke her ankle, she had to have the bed brought downstairs and the nurses in every day to help her.

They were supposed to put her to bed, but no way would she let them. That was my job. I'd pick her up and put her in the bed - it didn't matter what time I finished work, I'd pick Marg up, we'd head over there and I'd put her gran into bed - she wouldn't let anybody else do it. *I'm waiting for my mate Mac,* she'd say, and that's how it was. She were a biggish lady, but when you picked her up you could hear her bones cracking. I'd put her in bed, and then Marg and I would go home and have some dinner.

Marg's dad were a Dunkirk veteran, and he were a bit stand-offish with me at first, but that were because he knew my dad and he knew what my dad were like with other women. He were worried I might be the same. The apple don't fall far from the tree and all that. But I proved him wrong, and we got on really well after that.

He didn't talk about Dunkirk, except to say that he was some kind of clerk in the army, and as they retreated he'd carried this typewriter with him for miles and miles and miles, and when they were on the beach, waiting to be took off, his sergeant says to him *You can't take that with you.* And he remembered smashing it up with the butt of his rifle, because he weren't letting anybody else have it.

That were all he ever said about it. He weren't one to go on about things, but he were ever such a nice guy. We got on really well. I used to go over and dig his garden, because he couldn't, and set it with taters and beans and we'd go halves on what come off it.

Marg and I looked after him when he were poorly, when he had a triple heart bypass. Well, we think it were a triple heart bypass. He never said, because he weren't one to go on about things, as I've said. All I know is, he had a scar the length of his chest when he came out of hospital. He got right again, went back to work for a while, and then he took early retirement. He banked his money on the Wednesday, and on the Saturday he died in his sleep, and Marg's gran had died a few months before, and that was her family gone. From then on, it was her and me, but that wasn't always easy...

When I started wrestling, and got that full date sheet, Marg and me were like ships in the night. A lot of the time I'd get home from work, shower, change and be heading out just as she was coming in from her work, and we'd pass on the path. Then - depending on where I'd had to travel back from - it'd be anything from midnight to 3am before I got back. I'd climb into bed, fall fast asleep, get up for work the next morning, and do the same thing all over again. Marg has said since it was a very lonely life, because she was stuck at home on her own, and I were out wrestling. I think, if I'm honest, most wrestlers' wives felt the same, and said the same, if you bothered to ask them.

There were odd shows where I did take Marg with me. If I were travelling up on my own I'd take her - and if another wrestler's wife were there at the show she'd sit with them. She made quite a few friends, but whenever she came along I'd never speak to her.

That might sound rough, but I knew that if people knew Marg were with me they'd have a go at her to get at me. I'd see her sitting in the crowd, but I wouldn't acknowledge her, because they'd have a go. Punters were terrible in them days, not like now. Watch some of the old *World of Sport* wrestling and you'll see the difference in a wrestling crowd then from a wrestling crowd now. Back then, they'd lynch you, given half a chance.

The way we lived wouldn't have been everyone's cup of tea, but it suited the two of us. I was fine, Marg was fine, and it was what it was. We supported each other, and that was that. In the following years, when wrestling took me abroad, Marg never had any problems with me going. She didn't like it, but she'd always say *You go. Enjoy yourself, you might not get this opportunity again.*

She always backed me.

Her dad backed me, too - mostly - but there was one exception. He weren't over keen on me wrestling, but he'd never been to it, so one time I took him to a show I done with Pat Patton at Nuneaton, over at Bramcote army barracks. Her dad were chuffed to be coming along, but then I got disqualified for dropping Pat - straddle-legged - on the top rope. Marg's dad was furious. He never spoke to me all the way back to Mancetter. Next day, he gave me both barrels.

I'm disgusted with you!
Why?
What you done last night!
What?
I thought you were better than that!
It were...er... an accident.
It weren't an accident!
But...
It was disgusting!!
It were...
You done it on purpose!

I had done it on purpose, of course. I'd not been wrestling that long, and I knew that if I'd convinced him, I'd done my job right and I was on the right road. So I agreed with him that I'd let myself down, but really I was just trying to keep a straight face.

Marg's dad never went to the wrestling again.

Putting It In A Bit

Every time I went out on the road - which was every night - I was learning more about wrestling and how it worked. I learned that Max Crabtree might have four or five shows across the country of an evening - and one of them would be sure to feature his brother Shirley, who the world knew as Big Daddy - and that meant someone else would be in charge. It might be Jeff Kaye, an ex-wrestler, or Brian Crabtree who'd be refereeing or MCing if Max wasn't there. But whoever was senior would have the wages.

The ring would turn up in five or six big vans, like furniture vans. A bunch of lads would set the ring up, take it down afterwards, and drive it away. Wrestlers didn't touch it, not like nowadays. You just turned up and did the show. And the show was four matches, and it'd be finished by half nine, quarter to ten latest. That way, folk could catch the last buses home - a lot of people caught the bus, because fewer people had cars - so the formula was four matches per show.

The first match was a bit of cowboys and indians. By which I mean villainry. A little bit of that. Second match up would be a wrestling match, to bring the crowd down a bit, so a technical match with lots of holds, and the like. Then the third match would be your main event, the one that got the crowd worked right up, screaming and hollering. And the last match? Well, one of Max's favourite sayings was *Send them home happy!*

That meant the fourth match would be cowboys and indians again, but this time the blue eye would come out on top. As a heel, I think that was wrong. To my way of thinking, if the villain won the last match everyone would remember, and they'd want to come back next time to see him beat. But I may be biased, being a heel myself, and Max was the multi-millionaire out of the two of us, so I guess he knew what he was doing.

Most matches were six five-minute rounds. If it were a bigger match, like a championship or something, then it could be twelve or fifteen rounds, but they'd be three minutes each. You'd also got the rules. And you need the rules. A good villain needs rules he can break so he can get the crowd riled up. Break the rules, and you'd get a public warning. Break them again, and you'd get another. A third warning, and you'd be disqualified.

Warnings were part and parcel of being a villain. If I punched someone, the referee would give me a warning. A bit later on I might get a public warning. What would happen then is that the blue-eye would get a bit anxious and maybe punch me, so he'd get a public warning. That'd make the crowd really wild. And I'd stand there laughing. Which made them wilder still. That helped being a villain a lot. And it'd be two falls, two submissions, or a knockout to finish.

There was none of this high-flying acrobatics you get now. The only ones who did that were Dynamite Kid, Rocco, and British Bulldog. Dynamite would come off the top rope and do a headbutt. The rest of us stuck to cowboys and indians, and working the crowd. My role as a heel was to get them riled up by doing villainry, and then the blue eye would bring them down by getting out of it somehow. Then I'd do some more villainy to get them worked up again, and maybe a bit later he'd be the hero and turn the tables. That's how it was. You worked the crowd.

Every match was different. And everyone went home happy.

Very quickly, my favourite move became the splash. That was my finish - and it did finish things. I enjoyed that. My other speciality was the squash in the corner, especially if it was a tag match. We'd send the opponent into the corner, and then my partner would send me in to him. They'd drop out of the corner to the canvas, I'd splash them. Game over.

The move I didn't like being done on me were the leg lock. I've only got short legs anyway, and if someone put a leg lock on me - where they cross your legs and hook their leg in and pull back with it - it used to kill my knees. That was very uncomfortable.

Apart from that, I didn't mind anything. The harder the better, for me. I like to feel it, know what I mean? And wrestlers from different parts of the country had different styles. The London lads were very light in their wrestling. The northern lads liked you to put it in a bit. I learned the difference when me and Mal Kirk went down to London. We were up against Tom Tyrone - who were a good well-built lad, ever such a nice chap - and Big Daddy.

It was still early days for me, and I hadn't worked with the London lads before, so when Mal Kirk says to me *These London lads like you to put it in a bit* I took it at face value. Me and Tom Tyrone get in the ring, he does all his fancy stuff and gets the crowd clapping, and then... I can't think what I done to him... I think I hit him in the back, and all you heard was *Fackin 'ell!!*

Mal Kirk was stood in the corner laughing his socks off. As Tom stood up, he pulled me in, dragged me along to where Mal was, and said *You told him to do that, dint ya?* as if you couldn't tell anyway, with Mal laughing like he was. Tom knew what had gone on, I learned my lesson, and we had a good match. I wrestled him a few times after that, and wherever we were, we always gave a good show, and sent the punters home happy.

Here in the Midlands, we're in the middle of the wrestling world, between the northern lads - who were all into their amateur wrestling and would stick it in - and the southern lads who didn't like you to touch them too much, liked it light. That meant we could fit in with both. I could go up north and put it in the same as they did, and then I could go down south and work like them.

It was harder for southern lads to wrestle northerners. They didn't like it at all. There was a bit of friction between the two groups, I suppose. Don't get me wrong, the southern lads - Dave Bond, Ron Marino, Mal Saunders, Pete Roberts - they'd all done amateur as well, so they were rough. Lee Bronson could rip your head off if he wanted to. They were light, but they knew what they were doing. Don't for a moment think that they didn't.

It's just that everything was different down south from up north. If you got on the wrong side of Lee Bronson, you'd know it. He still does amateur wrestling even now, and he's in his seventies, but he'll go and have a pull round at the amateur clubs. Amateur wrestling is all about falls and submissions. Sometimes they'll start on their hands and knees and you've got to try and wrestle them over. It's an art. And once they've got a hold on you that's it. They could snap your arm or your leg, anything.

The lads down south could do it if they wanted to – they just didn't want to. it was funny the difference between the two groups. We benefitted from being able to wrestle both styles – light or putting it in – and because the M1 would take us south, the M6 would take us north. Geographically, we were in the right place. And style-wise, it worked for us too.

I don't think I ever had any complaints about the way I wrestled. And I got the work, so I must have been doing something right. I just kept doing what I knew I could do. I found my way to do it, and I done it and done it and done it for forty years. That's good going.

Just twelve months or so after I'd got in the ring at Brent, green as you like and wet behind the ears, I was at the top. I was wrestling Big Daddy, and tagging with Stacks, travelling up and down the country, and grabbing my sleep when I could.

In part, that was down to the lucky break of Johnny England getting sacked and me getting his date sheet so soon after I'd started, but it was also because I turned up to every single one of this dates, however tired I was, wherever I was supposed to be, and I always gave 100%. Every time.

Each month, my date sheet was full.

Every single day I was out wrestling.

Kay Fabe and Hard Cash

There's one thing that absolutely stands out about how wrestling was back then - you never ever ever talked about the business, about what goes on behind the show. We called it *kay fabe*, which is carney talk. This made sure that nobody got in who shouldn't, and nobody outside the world of wrestling knew anything. We used carney a lot, and cockney rhyming slang, too, so the outside person didn't know what we were talking about. Strangers who came in the changing room were *queens*. Nothing to do with being homophobic, but it was Queen's Park Rangers = strangers.

On one of the wrestling pages online recently, someone said to another bloke *You're nothing but a queens, really*. And the fella says *What do you mean a queens?* And the first guy replies *Well if you don't know, you don't know wrestling, do you? So I ain't saying no more.*

And back then it was all like that. You'd never talk to anybody about what went on, or what didn't go on.

It was part of the attraction. This idea you were in a secret society, a club with rules, and codes, and its own language. Every now and then you'd get somebody leaking it out to the papers - generally because they'd fallen out with Max and weren't getting any work. Banger Walsh did it once. He went to the papers and said *When they want some blood, you get paid £3 to cut your head open.* After that I got asked it a lot.

You cut your head open for £3? Is that right?

My answer was always the same.

Hang on, I'll go in my case.
Eh?
See if I've got a razor blade in my razor.
Why?
I'll give it you, I'll give you £3.00...
Er...
And you can cut your head open.
Oooh, no! I ain't doing that!
Well what makes you think I'm gonna do it then?

And everything carried on as it was.

Two or three people tried to expose the job like that. And once they'd done it, there was no way back in. We went to Leamington not long after Banger had, and he turned up. Three of us had to drag Terry Rudge off him. He nearly killed him for what he'd done. I can't understand what Banger was thinking, turning up. Because somebody would have done it. If Terry hadn't done it, it would have been somebody else.

It'd be like, if you dobbed your mate in for something, you'd expect your mate to have a go at you, wouldn't you? This was the same. The wrestling world was such a close-knit family that it took you a while to get in and get established, but once you were in, you were in. They'd do anything for you, they'd watch your back, they'd always have your back.

And let's get one thing straight: each and every one of us wrestled because we loved wrestling. None of us did it for the money, because you couldn't live on what we got. I always - even when I was at the top of the bill, and on TV - I always had a daytime job as well as being a wrestler. You couldn't make a living full-time with the wrestling, not really.

For that first match in Brent, I got a fiver. When Pat Patton had a word, I got a fiver plus petrol money. After one year as a professional wrestler, I was top of the bill, and getting paid about £10 a match. Even when I finished working for Max in 1994 I were getting just £25 for each match. Does this mean there was no money in wrestling?

No. It just means it wasn't ending up with us.

Let's take that match in Brent as an example. There were, say, 200 people in the audience, paying £2.50 a pop. That's £500 coming in. Andy and me were on £5.00 each, there's a tenner gone. The others might have been on £20, so that's maybe £100 on wrestlers for the night. There's hall hire, of course, but Max might have got it free, being as he was bringing in a lot of punters who'd drink. So £350-400 profit. Then there's five shows a night across the country, that's two grand. Multiply that by 90 days... and you're ending up with a fair whack of money.

For the TV shows, if I remember rightly, Max got twenty-five or thirty grand for them. Us? We got an extra £5.00, and wrestling was on TV every week for thirty years....

He made a lot of money, Max did. Because wherever in the country Shirley went, the place were full. No matter what size the hall was, it were full. When him and Stacks did Wembley, I think there were three thousand there. If John Quinn was wrestling, it'd be the same, four maybe five thousand punters in. A lot of shows would be in front of a few hundred people, but once I worked my way up into the tags – and that was before the end of my first year as a wrestler – I was in the shows where the rooms were all full.

What did I get? What did any of the wrestlers get? If the show were on TV, £25 plus your expenses. If it were in the Albert Hall, you'd get an extra £10. That was it.

Even for Cup Final Day – which was one of the biggest TV events in the wrestling year, with a wrestling match beamed out just before they showed the game, so it was a prime TV spot – even for the huge event of Cup Final Day, you still got £25. If you were standby and they didn't use you, or your match went 'in the can' and they used it later, you got £15. And the money they made off it?

Unthinkable.

None of that's a complaint, by the way. I wrestled because I loved wrestling, and the money I got from it paid for the little extras for me and Marg, nothing more. The wrestling money weren't anything, really. Unless you did the driving you weren't really making much at it, and doing the driving only made it half-decent. Marg and I didn't move to a big house or anything, but wrestling did make life a bit more comfortable. I got a new car, because I'd got to have a reliable car, seeing as I was travelling all over the country to wrestle every day that came.

What can I say? It was a good life, and I loved it.

Less than twelve months after I stepped into the ring in Brent I was topping the bill. Every night I was wrestling in front of 6-700 people, and that was a big difference – the noise level went up exponentially, and that made the adrenalin rush all the more, just like the first time in front of 200 people in Brent.

I never got any complaints about the way I worked or what I done. The only complaints were off the punters, and that were good. That meant I was doing my job right. Max would think that was brilliant.

I was working days at the quarry and doing the wrestling at night, and life was good.

It was really, really good.

Receipts

Whenever you talk about wrestling, there's one question people always want to ask.

Is it fixed?

The answer's no, but it's vital you know how far to go. It's like judo, or karate, or any contact sport or martial art. Let me explain...

If I was in the ring tonight and broke somebody's arm, and tomorrow night I broke somebody's leg, we've got a problem. Several problems, in fact. One: at the end of the month there's nobody to wrestle, because they're all laid up at home with limbs in plaster. Two: nobody will want to wrestle you - why would they get in the ring with you when they're going to end up out of commission for several weeks? Three: audiences won't come to see it.

It's the same with judo or karate: competitors have got the skills to break your arm or leg or whatever, but they know how far to go, how much pressure they can apply, and how to stop before something goes snap. Wrestling's exactly like that. If someone's got you in an armlock, they could break your arm. But two minutes later, they could be in the same armlock and you could snap their arm. It's swings and roundabouts, and you know how far to go without hurting people.

But it does happen. You do get what we in the job call 'a receipt' if you've hurt somebody. Once it's 'maybe', and you might get the benefit of the doubt. The second time it's 'receipt coming', and it's going to come back your way. That's the way it was. One time I wrestled Alan Kilby, the deaf and dumb bloke, at Benn Hall, Rugby. His speciality was the roundhouse kick, but he never watched where his kick was landing. And this night at Benn Hall, he hit me right in the throat.

Of course, I couldn't breathe. I went down on my knees and I was gasping for breath. I think it was Jeff Kaye who was refereeing, and he hit me on the back to get me to breathe again. Then, as it happened, the bell went for the end of the round. I got in my corner, and Jeff came over, asked *Are you all right to carry on?* I said I was. He says, *I know what's coming now.*

I said *Yep. I hope he does.*

The bell went for the start of the next round, I got Alan in the middle of the ring, grabbed him by the hair, pulled him in, and hit him smack in the nose. Split all his nose, and gestured to him with my fingers 'one each'. He was trying to say *Why? Why?* because he could say the odd word, more or less. And I gestured again, and he knew. What had made it worse, and why I'd seen red, was that when he hit me in the throat he'd stood there laughing at me as I gasped for air. That's why Jeff said to me *I know what's coming.* He knew. That was how it was.

And it was great entertainment for the punters, too. When I punched Alan in the nose it really got the crowd going. They thought he'd finished me, but then I'd hit him back and split his nose - and done it in a way the referee couldn't see - and that really got the heat going. They hated me even more then. They probably went home talking about it, and woke up talking about it next day. And that's good for business. They'll come and see you next time you're in town, too, and boo you even louder and hate you even more. But the injuries were real. You can't fake being kicked in the throat, or getting your nose split.

And when we got out of the ring?

Me and Alan were fine with each other. It was job done. Bygones are bygones. Finished. Like I say, that was how it was. I could have a good match with anybody. The rules, and a villain to break them, and a good blue eye to die, were key. A blue eye mustn't just die, he's got to have his comebacks, where he stops the villain and gets the crowd going, so the villain can then stop him to bring them down again, and then when he's ready, the blue eye comes back again.

A good match would be two people who knew their job. I did one match - and this was still early days, and all my matches till then had been with Pat Patton - where we went down to Bath and I were on with Clive Myers, the British arm-wrestling champion. He'd been in a Sylvester Stallone film where Stallone was a trucker who did arm-wrestling, and Clive were in that film too, because he'd showed him how to do it.

I said to Pat, what's he like to work with? And Pat said, depends what mood he's in. I thought, *Right... here we go...*

By then I was 23-24 stone, and Clive were only a thin lad, maybe half my weight. I went in the changing rooms and spoke to him, and he kind of grunted back and never spoke to me again. So I left it. I never bothered him. Then, not long before we were due to come out, he came over and said what fall he'd be doing and when he'd be doing it. And I said, OK. Nice and quiet.

We got in the ring, the bell went, and we circled round. Then we went to link up, like I did with Pat, and he put his thumb straight in my eye. I thought *Bastard.* So then I just mauled him around for six rounds. He should have got his fall in the fourth, but I mauled him around for the full six rounds, and the match finished as a draw. We got back in the changing rooms, and Clive wasn't happy. What had happened? Why hadn't I let him get his fall? I told him straight

You know what happened. When we linked up you put your thumb in my eye. And you knew you'd done it, so don't say you didn't. So I made you look as much of an arsehole as I was, because you couldn't do anything with me, because I was too big. Next time - I said - *next time, hopefully, we'll have a good match.*

And we did. I wrestled him three or four times after that and it were brilliant. But that time, he took a liberty, so I took one back. That's the code. And he took a liberty because I was a new lad, and he thought he'd get away with it.

There was a real old-school code about wrestling back then. If you ask me, it was a lot harder in those days than it is now, and I mean no disrespect in saying that. You learned your bumps without crash mats, on a concrete floor, from older wrestlers who saw you as a potential threat to their own living, and made life hard for you as a consequence.

If you stuck with it, you learned your trade, and then you went in the ring, and travelled up and down the country seven nights a week, living on next to no sleep, for less money than you might expect we got.

And you did it because wrestling was in your blood, as simple as that.

Injuries

Injuries are part and parcel of life as a professional wrestler. Pat Roach picking me up and throwing me onto a concrete floor as part of my training had shown me that, right at the start. When I were out on the road I'd always be coming back home with black eyes and bruises, like every wrestler gets. That were just part and parcel of the job.

In all the years I spent wrestling, I only had two really bad injuries.

The first one were on my right leg. I banged it - don't ask me how - and the outside of my leg swelled right up. My mate were an ambulance man. He took a look and said I should go to the hospital. I thought it was nothing to worry about and it'd go down. It didn't. It got bigger.

One Sunday morning he called round, purely to check on my leg, and I hadn't even got up. I had to come downstairs on my bum, because I couldn't put any weight on my leg. He said *Right, I'm taking you down the hospital.* He took me down, and got me seen straight away. The nurse didn't like the look of my leg either, and she got a doctor to take a look at it. *Oh,* he says, *it's only fluid. Give him some tablets, and send him home. He's been walking on his leg too much.*

George, my mate, pipes up and tells him how I had to come down the stairs on my bum and couldn't put any weight on my leg at all, but this doctor doesn't want to know.

The sister ignored him and fetched another doctor. He took a look at it and said *Have you had anything to eat?* I said I hadn't. *Good, because we're going to operate on you.*

They took me straight down to theatre, and when they lanced this lump the pus squirted out with such force it hit the ceiling. I'd had an ingrowing abscess, and it was so big they filled a bowl with pus, and there was still more on the ceiling. They packed the cavity in my leg so it'd heal from the inside, and then every day I had to go back and have it changed. As it got better, the nurse would visit at home to change it, and then after a while it was down to me. I asked Marg if she would, and she said

No, I can't do that.

Which was fair enough. So I did it myself, pushing packing into my leg with a cotton bud. I kept doing that, day after day, till it more or less healed. Then I went back to the hospital. I saw an African doctor, who took a look at my leg and said *I don't like the look of that.* And he started smelling it. I thought *What's going on here?*

He said *No, I don't like the look of that, it don't look right to me.* And he gripped the sides of the wound, pulled them apart and opened it up again. *There you are. Look.* And all this pus run out again. It were infected inside.

After I'd come down off the ceiling and called him everything under the sun, I had the wound packed once more. All in all it took about 13-14 weeks to heal. I couldn't wrestle - because the wound was right where the top of my wrestling boots would rub against it - but I still went to work at the quarry. A man's got to earn a living.

The injury I got at Stockport was the one that stopped me doing anything. It nearly stopped me completely. We'd gone up in my car, me and Lucky Gordon the mad Irishman, with Marg and Lucky's daughter Sophia. Lucky were in the first match, and I were in the tag with Drew McDonald against Big Daddy and Ray Steele.

We were a couple of rounds in, and I was stood on the outside of the ring, holding the ropes. Ray Steele run over, grabbed me by the back of the neck, and went to pull me over the ropes into the ring. As I went over, I made a really bad mistake - I let go of the ropes. If I'd have held onto them, I'd have somersaulted over into the ring and been all right. But for some reason I let go of them, and landed with my feet up in the air, and all my weight on the back of my neck.

I were out cold. Instantly.

Jeff Kaye was referee, and he stopped the match immediately so the first aiders could come over. He wouldn't let them touch me, because he thought I'd broken my neck, and was worried that if anyone moved me I could end up in a wheelchair or worse, so he wouldn't let them touch me. All I can remember when I came round was somebody saying *Don't go to sleep. Don't let him go to sleep.*

There was blood coming out of my ear. Drew McDonald went and found Marg and said to her *I think you'd better go down the side of the ring to him, because it's not looking very good.*

The ambulance crew came, and the police and the fire brigade, and none of them would touch me either. They sent for a doctor from the hospital. He came over, injected me – I don't know what with, I only know what Marg told me – and then he let them lift me about an inch off the canvas, and they slid this tarpaulin underneath me that the fire brigade had with them. Then they brought a pump-up bed from the local hospital – at the time they only had one, and they had to chuck somebody out of it, so they could use it for me – and once the ropes had been taken off the ring and they could get it to the side of the ring, they pumped it up to the same height and slid me straight onto this bed.

What happened next were like something out of a *Carry On* film, because the ambulance men and the fire brigade had to push me through the streets of Ashton-under-Lyme all the way to the hospital. Really. They got me in the hospital, caught their breath, and sent me for X-rays. They'd take an X-ray, develop it and look at it, decide they could move me a bit and take another X-ray from a different angle, and repeat the process. It took four hours before they decided I hadn't actually broken my neck.

That was a huge relief all round.

Lucky Gordon drove Marg back home in my car, and

I lay there in hospital on a hospital bed, with sandbags at each side of my head so I couldn't move it. I don't know what they'd pumped me full of, but it was as if I were floating, as if I weren't there, lying stuck between all these sandbags, unable to move my head, only able to move my eyes. And all through the night I'd hear nurses going *Is he in here? Is that wrestler in here?* and then coming in to see me, because what had happened had been on the TV news.

My first thoughts when I realised what had happened were that I'd never walk again. A neck injury, that can be bad. If you're unlucky, it can paralyse you, and I didn't think I could cope with that. It was a relief to learn next day that all I'd done was rip all the nerves and the muscles in my neck.

All I'd done. By then I'd say I weighed 32 stone, and that's a lot of weight to land on your neck. I were in there four or five days, and Marg visited me every day. I never heard nothing from Max. Nothing at all.

All this happened just before Xmas, and at one point they'd been on about transferring me down to Nuneaton hospital so I could spend Xmas there, but in the end they let me out the day before Xmas Eve – *as long as you do as you're told* – with a big collar on so I couldn't move my neck. Lucky Gordon come up and drove me home, bless him, and I spent twelve weeks at home with the collar on.

How much looking after did I need when I got home? Not too much, because I could do more or less everything I needed to, just slowly, and without any sudden movements. Once I could walk, and go to the toilet, I knew I'd be OK. I'd been given a load of neck exercises to do, and they were hard at first, because of the pain, but once I started doing them, they got easier. It were like training - the more you do it, the easier it gets. I kept doing my neck exercises just like I'd been told, and I were all right. I got through it.

I got through it, but the enforced sitting around drove me crazy. It done my head in. I weren't used to sitting about. I were always working, wrestling, doing something.

When I'd had the leg abscess I'd still kept working at the quarry, but this time I couldn't. I'd just got to put up with it, but it were really hard, and money were a bit scarce. Marg were working - a good job she was, really - and once she come home of an evening I were all right, because then I had company. But during the day, on my own, it drove me crazy. I don't know how Marg did it when I was away, because now it was me wearing those shoes, and it weren't nice.

The nurses and doctors done a brilliant job and I can't thank them enough. Marg was a star. Max never got in touch. Then twelve weeks after the accident, about five minutes after I'd taken the collar off for the last time, the phone rang.

How you doing?
I'm OK now.
Good. We've got a show at Coalville.
When?
Tonight.

Oh.
Can you do it?

Like a fool, I says yeah. So I drive over to Coalville with my stomach churning over. I walk through the doors and I'm in the tag with Shirley. I get changed and get in the ring and part of me's on automatic pilot, doing what I've always done, and another part of me is looking round to see where the exit doors are, thinking

What the hell am I doing here??!!

and wondering whether I could do a runner, whether I should do a runner. And just as I was deciding the best thing to do was bolt, Shirley's music started and he got in the ring, and in that moment the adrenalin kicked in and all the nerves just went.

It's amazing, really, that when you've had something like that happen, you can still get back in the ring and undo it. As I say, up until Shirley's music started playing, I were looking for somewhere to run to. But once his music were playing and he got in the ring with me, the adrenalin kicked in and I never thought about it again.

I was back into wrestling, and life was back to normal.

BIG DADDY PRAYED FOR RIVAL

GENTLE giant Big Daddy revealed last night how he knelt down and prayed for an injured opponent.

30st GRAPPLER GETS THE GIANT HEAVE-HO!

Plight of a groaning wrestler

RESCUE workers had to call in the heavy mob when 30-stone grappler Scrubber Daly hurt his back in a wrestling match.

For it needed TEN men to carry the injured heavyweight to a nearby hospital

KO for a ring king

The drama started before the timekeeper's going had chance to ring. As the man mountain heaved himself into the ring, he fell across the ropes head downwards.

"Scrubber" — real name MacDonald Hardiman — lay there in agony as worried officials sent for the emergency services.

It took four ambulancemen, five firemen, seven police officers, a doctor and a nurse to lift him.

Big Mal falls foul of weight

Wife at ringside sees injury

LIFTED

all over the papers...

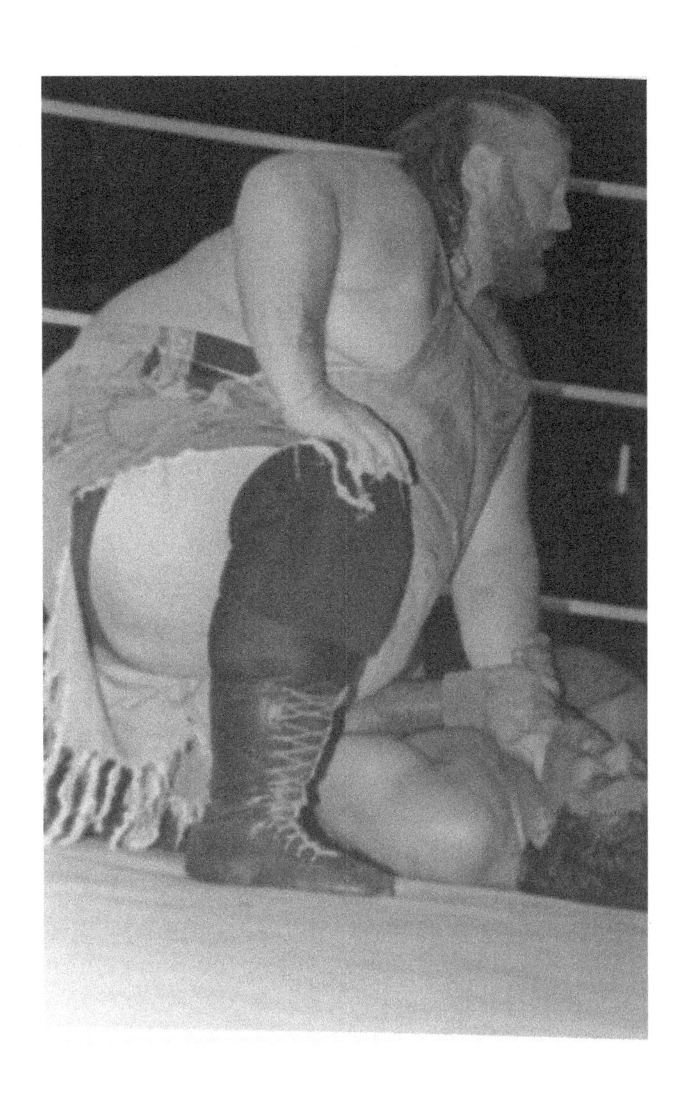

then back in the ring...

Shirley and Mal

It was another night, wrestling in Croydon, when I broke Big Daddy's arm. I'd been wrestling three or four years by then, and we were in a tag match. Me and Banger Walsh - who'd somehow made his peace with Max and come back to wrestling - against Pat Patton and Daddy.

It's the start of the match, and me and Banger are already in the ring. Then Pat Patton jumps in. Daddy's still messing about outside it, whooping the crowd up. Now, I'm a heel, and my take on it is that if somebody gets in the ring, and there's two of you in there, you set about him. Get your villainry in early. So I do. I knock Pat about, pick him up, and chuck him over the ropes. But Shirley's stood on the floor with his arm on the edge of the ring, and Pat lands right on Shirley's arm and snaps it.

Throwing Pat out of the ring was all part and parcel of being a heel, it was me doing my job. I hadn't even realised Shirley was standing there when I threw Pat out. But when I heard the crack of Shirley's arm breaking - and it was very loud, so loud a lot of the punters must have heard it - I thought

I'm going to get it now, for sure. Here comes an empty date sheet.

What happened next? Well, we did the match, believe

it or not. Shirley carried on, and we just had to adapt to the fact that he had a broken arm. When we got back to the changing room afterwards, I thought I'd cop for it then, but Max were fine. He said *Just one of them things, kid.* He always called you kid. *He'll be back tomorrow.*

Two days later, I wrestled Daddy again. I was surprised to see him, to be honest, but the lads told me he'd wrestled the night before, with his arm in plaster. He could get away with it, couldn't he? And he was fine with me when we got in the ring - this was in Skegness - he never mentioned it, there was no animosity, nothing. I knew there wouldn't be a receipt coming for what I'd done, because I didn't do it on purpose. If I'd done it on purpose, that would have been different, I would have expected a receipt. Everyone knew what had happened, and everyone were fine with it.

It were one to me, I suppose. Heat of the moment, out Pat went, and bang went Shirley's arm. He didn't get injured a lot, really. It were very rare he had a night off. I can't remember him having a night off, tell you the truth, and most times, you were wrestling seven nights a week. In winter, it might be five or six nights a week and Sunday off. Shirley lived out of a suitcase, really, bless him. According to form, even when he had his stroke, Max fetched him out of bed. That were after I'd finished. I didn't see that, and I'm glad I didn't, because someone like Shirley should have been let retire with dignity, not brought out like that just for making money.

It might seem a bit of a surprise that Banger was back wrestling after falling out with Max in public, but Banger were what they call Daddy fodder. He'd be the one who did all the stupid bumps with Shirley. Like the back elbows.

With those, Shirley would send Banger into the corner. Then, when he came staggering out, Shirley would bend down, so Banger was lying on Shirley's back with his head down the middle of his back. He'd hook Banger's arms in, and stand up. Banger's upside down now, with his feet in the air, his head down near the middle of Shirley's back, his arms hooked through Shirley's so he can't go anywhere, and then Shirley drops back on top of him, lays him out.

I've seen times where - after the back elbows - Banger didn't know who he was or where he was, whether it were Xmas or Easter or a week last Wednesday.

Most wrestlers wouldn't do the back elbows with Shirley. I did it once, just once, but I wouldn't do it again. I admit he looked after me, he didn't hurt me, but when Max wanted it again, I said no. Max weren't giving it up that easy, though *Why? It looked good, kid.* I had to think on my feet, and I had the perfect answer.

He can't lift thirty-six stone up like that every night. I'm not doing it. It'll kill him. I'm not having that on my conscience.

Max nodded, and I never did back elbows again. Banger was fifteen or sixteen stone, so that were different, and he were always there to take the silly bumps with Shirley. They'd put him in a tag team with Stacks or me or Mal Kirk, and Banger would be the one taking the silly bumps. That's how it worked. They always put a smaller guy in with Shirley, and he took the beatings. Banger was always the smaller guy with the villains, so he took all the silly bumps.

Thing is, there were a lot of Shirley to fall on you, and however careful he was - and like I say, he looked after me the one time I did the back elbows, and made sure not to hurt me - there was always going to be an element of risk. Mal Kirk, who was an ex-rugby league player based in Wigan, died in the ring with Shirley. Actually, he didn't. They got him back into the dressing room and he died there, for all the difference it makes.

I'd wrestled Mal a lot over the years. He were a big man, and he loved his beer. Specifically, he loved his Tetleys. He'd always got to get home for his Tetleys. When he finished a show his catchphrase was *It's Tetleys time!* He were a really really nice guy, but he was wrestling Shirley in Great Yarmouth, Shirley splashed him, and Mal hit the floor and didn't get up.

They managed to get him out of the ring and back to the dressing room, but there were nothing they could do. Mal's heart had stopped. He was fifty-one years old.

I should have been there that night, but I'd not been able to go. Instead, I were out on my milk round at 4 o'clock on the Monday morning, and I heard on the radio that Mal had died.

And I just had to go home. I left the lad to finish the milk round for me, and went home. I were devastated. Mal had taught me so much, and helped me so much when I was starting out.

Everybody on the wrestling scene was shocked and hurting. But the wrestlers who'd been in the show at Yarmouth were out wrestling the following night. What happened to Mal didn't stop Shirley doing splashes. And it didn't stop me doing splashes either. It turned out Mal had a heart condition, and could have died at any time, and we just put it down as one of those unfortunate things that happens, and nothing to do with Shirley doing the splash on him.

The show went on.

Punters

Punters back in the day used to have a real go at you. I wrestled a lot at Bedworth, which is two or three mile outside Nuneaton. They hated me there, because I was a villain. I've always said, the more people that hate me, the more I know I'm doing my job properly. And in Bedworth, even if I weren't wrestling, if I went to the Civic Hall, it went deathly quiet when I walked in the bar. I kind of liked that. You get a buzz out of it.

I was doing a tag match at Bedworth once. It were me and Mal Kirk against Shirley and Pat Patton, and I were standing on the outside of the ring. I'd been in with Pat and given him a good beating, and then I'd tagged Mal and he'd gone in. So I was standing on the outside of the ring, and this woman run down from where she was sitting and clawed me down the back of my legs.

She broke every nail on her fingers. Every single one. And I'd got ten bleeding score marks down the back of my legs, five on each leg. This woman was an ex-headmistress at my secondary school. She'd just retired. She must have been sixty, sixty-five years old.

Now, headmistress of a secondary school, that's a fairly prestigious position - and here she was, scratching my legs for all she was worth. It wasn't nice - of course it wasn't nice - but I knew if I'd got someone like her into that kind of state, I'd done my job.

Again.

Another time, early in my career, it were me and Mal Kirk again, at Hanley in Stoke-on-Trent. It was the first time I'd been there. As we're about to head out from behind the stage curtains into the ring, Mal says to me

You go that side, the left-hand side.
Why?
Just go the left-hand side.
OK...

Mal was smirking, and I knew there had to be something going on but I couldn't think what. I was still puzzling about it as we walked out, and I got this *Whack!* on top of my head. Mal were killing himself laughing. There was a woman who sat in the balcony, and in her handbag she always carried a big pot of Vaseline. The highlight of her evening was hitting wrestlers on the head with it if they got close enough.

And she cracked my head open.

We'd about finished this match, and a woman runs down to the ring with her shoe in her hand and hits me with the heel as hard as she can, right across the top of my foot. When I got back to the dressing room, I took my boot off, and my foot just swelled up like a balloon. It had a big comedy egg on it. I'd got to drive back to Nuneaton, and I couldn't get my shoe on over this lump. In the finish, I had to tape my shoe to the bottom of my foot so I could walk to my car and drive home.

After I'd been in wrestling a bit, I realised that the women punters were worse than the men. They knew you weren't going to hit them back, so they'd go for it. It were unbelievable the way they'd have a go at you. Men were a bit more wary. They probably thought they'd get a smack in the nose. Although we couldn't. If I'd have hit them, I'd have got done. If they got in the ring, that was different, they were in my territory. But outside the ring, you couldn't. Or let's say, you couldn't do anything obvious. You had to box a bit clever.

I was wrestling at St Albans once, in a singles against Alan Kilby. To build the tension before a match, the venue would dim the room lights, and just light the steps we'd come down. Everything else was black. I were coming down the steps, and this guy put his foot out and tripped me up. He was sitting with five or six women, and he thought he'd look smart. He started laughing. I let it go. I knew at one point or another, I'd get my own back. I did a couple of rounds with Kilby, and in the third round I chucked him out of the ring and followed him round the room, belting him. We were heading toward the guy who'd tripped me, and I knew he were going to stand up. He'd just got to. So I stood Kilby up right in front of this bloke, drew back my fist, saw the bloke stand, and as I went to punch Kilby I pulled his head down, and hit this bloke straight in the face. He went four rows back.

Oh, mate, I'm ever so sorry!

That was for the benefit of the crowd. I went over and picked him up, saying *I'm ever so sorry, he ducked!* And as I pulled him up I got my mouth by his ear and said

That'll teach you to be so fucking cocky. His nose was all smashed. The women he was with got up and left him.

You could always work it so you got your own back. It's part of the job, I think. And the lesson is simple: if you don't want to get on the wrong side of a wrestler, don't do it. You'd think that'd be obvious, but people do. They have a few drinks, think they'll be cock of the north, and only learn the error of their ways when it's too late.

Like the time I was doing a tag, me and Pete Lapaque, outside at a village fete. There was six or seven guys, all been on the drink, all getting lippy. So I got lippy back, because nine times out of ten that'll put them back in their box. I said to one of them

Good job your mouth ain't the size of your nose. It'd be as big as the Mersey Tunnel.

He didn't like it, but that was his problem, not mine. The tag match finished, I was stood in the corner chatting to Pete, and he looks over my shoulder and says to me

He's in the ring.
You what?
That bloke, he's in the ring.

So I turn round, and there's this bloke. I look over to the promoter and ask him

What do you want me to do?
He's in the ring, you do what you've got to do.
Righto.

The fella charged at me. I moved, and I hit him. Forearmed him. His nose were pouring with blood. I picked him up, chucked him over the top of the ropes and out of the ring, and he landed on his back next to his mates' feet. *Right, who's next?* All of them sidled off. Two coppers had seen the whole thing, and after I'd got changed, and headed to my car, they came over. Was I about to get arrested? No. *We saw what you did, and we just want to thank you. It saved us having to lock him up.*

And that were that.

Then there was the time I was wrestling at Holbeach, in Lincolnshire. The crowd there was red-hot, every time. All night, it'd be bubbling. This particular night, it was me and Lucky Gordon against Dick Harrison - who run the show and who was obviously the local hero - and a young lad he'd brought in. We're doing this tag, and I get chucked out the ring. Physically chucked out. I'm standing on the floor, and this guy comes up behind me and kicks me in the backside. But he catches me right on my coccyx. The pain were like somebody had shoved a red-hot poker up my back, and he's stood there, laughing. Right then, his card were marked.

Whenever you wrestled tag at Holbeach - whoever you were with - when you left the ring you'd leave back-to-back so no-one could get behind you and hit you from behind. That's how hot the crowd at Holbeach were. If you didn't watch each other's backs on the way to the dressing room, you'd get thumped, simple as that. So this night, as me and Lucky are leaving the ring I say to him *When we're down in the crowd, I'll give you a nudge with my elbow. You spin round and give me a push, OK?*

We get down out of the ring, and there's the bloke, the one who kicked me. I give Lucky the nudge, he pushes me, and as I fall forward, I hit the bloke straight in the nose.

Bang. That's him dealt with.

I get changed, drive home, and pull up outside my house at two in the morning. There's a police car sitting there.

A copper gets out.

Mr Daley?
Yes?
You've just been to Holbeach?
Yes.
We've had a complaint.
Oh.
You've hit a bloke.
I have?
You've broke his jaw, fractured his eye socket...
Really?
But he hasn't been to the hospital...
He hasn't?
So I don't know how he works all that out.
I see.
Anyway...
Yes?
If you come down the station in the morning...
Right.
And bring me a signed photo for my grandson...
OK.
I can guarantee you you won't hear any more about it.

Next morning, I'm down the station with a signed photo, and sure enough I never hear anything more about it.

That was how it worked. Most of the time, anyway.

But if it didn't pan out that way, things could get really sticky. Let me tell you about one very scary moment, when it all went wrong.

Arrest

I was doing a show in Reading, at the Hexagon Centre, which is shaped like a threepenny bit. It was a tag event, with me and Stacks against Shirley and... I think it were Jackie Turpin. We're in the ring waiting for them to come in, and some bloke throws a bottle at me. It hits me in the face, I feel something running down my face and think it's blood, so I jump out of the ring, and chase him. He runs down the corridor to the changing rooms, where Shirley and Jackie were waiting to come in, and was caught like a rat in the trap.

I don't know what happened next, and I'm sure it was just a terrible accident, but one way or another he may have had a bit of a hiding.

The next day, he's spoken to *The Sun,* saying I'd attacked him. He'd also rung Max Crabtree. He admitted he'd thrown a bottle at me first, so Max said *Well, I ain't giving you any money, and I don't think Mr Daley will either.*

Then I get a phone call from Reading police station.

Mr Hardiman?
Yes.
You've got two choices.
OK...
You can come down on your own accord...
Uh-huh.

To Reading police station...

Or?

Or we will have to have you arrested and locked up till such time as we can get up to see you to interview you about this incident last night.

I'll come down.

I drove down to Reading, walked into the police station, and two CID blokes - who were ever so nice - ask me what had happened. I tell them what I remember. The one copper says

You ain't told me that. This is what happened. He threw the bottle, you chased after him, there was a load of chairs at the bottom of the corridor - which there were, because they'd been and checked - *and you being 28 stone couldn't stop, you run into him, and squashed him into the chairs. That's what really happened, isn't it?*

Er, yes. Yes, it is.

Good, he said. *Now we're off to arrest him for throwing the bottle. He's a troublemaker round Reading. We've been after him for a long while.*

I drove back home, pleased as punch, thinking that was the end of it. But it wasn't. A few days later, I get another phone call from them, telling me I'd have to go down to Reading again. It seemed the Crown Prosecution Service had chucked out the case against him, but wanted to prosecute me for causing actual bodily harm. So I drive down to Reading and the coppers tell me

We've got to arrest you. They arrest me, charge me, and I drive back home.

A month or so later, I'm driving back down to Reading to enter a plea in court. I get there and the bloke who threw the bottle is there, goading me, trying to get me to have a go at him again. Luckily, two coppers clear him off. *You're not supposed to be here, you're not involved in this,* they tell him. *On yer bike.* I go in to court, tell them what happened, plead not guilty, and drive back home again.

My solicitor says he'll get me a good barrister, and I trust him. So on the day of the hearing I'm back down to Reading once more. The barrister meets me, says *Can I have a word, Mr Hardiman?*

Uh-oh, this doesn't sound good.

I'm afraid, he says, *that your solicitor's interpretation of this case is different to mine. You're looking at a minimum of five years.*

I felt everything drain out of me. I hadn't expected that. I had to sit down. Things are looking way more serious than I'd ever imagined. If I'm convicted, Max will drop me like a hot brick. Being found guilty and sent to prison for violence against punters, that's beyond the pale. It's inexcusable.

We go into court, and I get a very lucky break. The bloke hasn't turned up. His barrister wants an adjournment, but every time she asks for something, my barrister stops her in her tracks. In the end, the judge says *I'll adjourn this case to after dinner. You've got an hour to get him here.*

It was the most nervous hour I think I've ever known. My next five years could hinge on what happens in this sixty minutes. I can't even think of eating anything. The court's about to reconvene, and the bloke still hasn't turned up. My barrister and his barrister are having a right argument in the corridor. They call us back in. She goes to make her case. The judge stops her.

Hold on. Before you speak, have you found him?
No. We can't find him anywhere.
Right. No case to answer. Case dismissed.

I'm up on my feet and out of the box, wanting to get out of the courtroom as quick as I can, because I've got visions of the bloke coming in through the door just as I think I'm out of this scot free. I'm on my way to freedom, and then my barrister says *Hold on, Mr Hardiman, can you just get back in the box a minute.*

What??!!

I say *Right ho,* thinking *For Christ's sake, just let me get out of here!* I get back in the box, and my barrister turns to the judge.

Mr Hardiman has been down to Reading three times now, and being as the plaintiff hasn't turned up, I think he should have his expenses paid. The judge agrees.

And I'm out of there, as fast as I can, in my car and out of Reading.

I never did get the expenses, either.

South Africa

I'd been able to get into wrestling because a bunch of mates had clubbed together for me to learn with Pat Roach. For my first match in Brent, I'd been paid £5.00. Three years later, in August 1988, I was on my first trip abroad, wrestling in South Africa for £100 a match, and being treated like a rock star. What wasn't to like?

For that first South Africa trip I flew straight from Heathrow to Johannesburg with Gil Singh, the Indian wrestler - he was like god over there - and as soon as we landed they took him away to do a TV interview in Capetown, and I went to where I was stopping in Johannesburg. I met up with the other wrestlers who'd be on the bill over the next few weeks, but they wouldn't talk to me. It was like that first match in Brent all over again, except this time I understood what was happening. We drove from Jo'burg to Durban for the first match, and I sat in a minibus with a bunch of guys who were all speaking Afrikaans and wouldn't say a word to me till I'd shown what I was made of.

They learned what I was made of all right. I was in South Africa to do four matches, and the first one was in Durban. We got there, and I was wrestling Gil Singh. During the match I splashed him, one of the boards broke, and it shot up and broke his ribs. That was it, game over. Gil couldn't wrestle any more, they had to stop the match so they could take him off to hospital, and the punters went absolutely crazy. They wanted to kill me, and if they could have got at me they just might have. So the organisers shut me in the changing rooms for my own safety, and left me there. Then they forgot I was there.

I waited and waited. Eventually I realised they'd gone home and forgotten me. At 3 o'clock in the morning I'm sat outside the venue on my own. I've no phone numbers to ring anyone, I've no money, I've nothing. I'm in a strange country, not knowing what's what, what I'm going to do next, just me and my bag with my kit in, and this car comes up the road. It stops. A bloke says *You one of the wrestlers?* I tell him that I am, and that I'm stuck there on my lonesome, with no phone numbers, no clue what to do. *Hang on* he says. And he rings someone, and they ask him to take me back to the hotel. I put a word in *While you're on the phone, tell them I'm fuckin' starving – I've had nothing to eat all day.*

The bloke drives me back to the hotel, I go up to my room, and ten minutes later there's a knock on my door. This bloke comes in with one big bucket of fried chicken, another bucket full of chips., and three big bottles of fresh orange. It was like the feeding of the five thousand. And I was that five thousand.

I had a good feast, had a good sleep, I get up next morning, go down for breakfast... and nobody would serve me. They're all talking about me – I know because they're all pointing at me – but literally nobody would come and serve me.

I go to the front desk and said to speak to the manager. The woman just looks at me and ignores me. *What the hell's going on here?* A man walks by, wearing a suit. I ask him if he's the manager.

Yeah... why?
Nobody will serve me.
Well, you put Gil Singh in hospital.
Eh?
That's why they won't serve you.

He's clearly not intending to do anything to change that, either. Luckily, the bloke who's driving me around walks in. I tell him what's going on, he has a few words with the manager in Afrikaans, I'm led back into the dining area, and they feed me. They're not very happy about it, though. They take their wrestling seriously here, and they don't like their gods having their ribs broken, either.

My second match was in Johannesburg. A tag match, with me and Lance von Erik teaming up against the South African champion and a wrestler in a mask - they liked to have a blue-eye in a mask - and the crowd is huge. There's maybe 30,000 people there. Stalls, a circle, an upper circle. A sea of faces every which way you looked, and they hated us because we were the heels and we were up against their champion. The promoter's already had a word with me.

Scrubber.
Yes?
I need you to rip 'em apart.

Really?
Yes.
In other words, you want a riot?
If you can cause a riot, then yes.
OK.

I know where I stand now. As we walk out from the changing rooms toward the ring, I stop to talk to this policeman who's on guard by the dressing room door. And while we're talking, I take his handcuffs off him. He knows I've done it, but he daren't say a thing. I put the handcuffs in my dungarees, and get in the ring. Lance knows I'm up to something, and he doesn't like it.

You're going to get us killed here.
Don't worry.
Don't worry??!!
It's only the last bit that hurts.

The other two wrestlers get in the ring, the crowd's right up, and even before the bell's gone to start the match, we're pushing and shoving each other. I push the South African champion into his corner, get the handcuffs out, and *Crikkk!* He's handcuffed. He can't do anything. He can't move. That's him dealt with – the copper daren't come down with the keys, because the crowd will kill him for letting me have the cuffs in the first place – and now I pick up the masked guy, splash him, and get back to working on the champion who's handcuffed in the corner. His head's all split open, there's blood everywhere. Lance gets in the ring with me, saying *I don't like this! I don't like this!* So I hit him, pick him up, slam him to the floor, and splash him. That's him finished, too. And for good measure, when the MC gets in, I slam and splash him as well.

By now, the promoter's got his riot. I've broken all the rules, every single one of them, and the crowd don't like it. They're throwing chairs. They're throwing ashtrays the size of waste-paper bins. They're throwing anything they can get their hands on. Chairs and ashtrays are flying off the upper circle balcony, and they're all aimed at me. Some bloke's helping me get back from the ring to the dressing room, and I've got my hands over my head to protect myself. As we get to the passageway that leads to the changing rooms, I think *Phew, I'm safe!* I lower my hands, and somebody drops one of these big ashtrays straight on my head and splits it open.

The place gets smashed to pieces. I'm locked in the changing rooms with my head streaming blood and my hands black and blue, while 30,000 people have a riot because they can't get at me for what I've done. There are two armed guards on the doors to stop them getting in, and I know it isn't going to be safe to get me out of here and take me back to the hotel until everybody's gone.

I'm grinning to myself. I've done my job. The promoter's got his riot, and now the South African wrestlers know what I'm made of.

From here on, they can't do enough for me - *Do you want something to eat, Scrubber? Would you like a drink?* - and I've still two more matches to do.

SPORT

FOR THE RECORD

Look Ma, I'm flying!

CRASH LANDING . . . Scrubber Dale (199 kgs) does a crash landing on fellow Briton Steve Ray (130 kgs) during their work-out at Goodwood yesterday, in preparation for their bouts on tonight's Worldwide Wrestling Promotion's tournament at Good Hope Centre. Tonight's full programme is: Tiger Singh v Steve Ray; Danie Voges v Steve Ray; Famous Lance v Jumbo Big Daddy; Kalahari Boerboel v Gregg Bragg and Abdul Kader v Trevor v d Westhuizen. Pic: Brenton Geach

Pictures: OBED ZILWA, The Argus

L HUNG UP: Anaconda the Giant had his problems (top) at the Good Hope ntre last night against Danny Voges . . . and after defeat by two falls to one, rubber Daly (above) jumped into the ring to register his own protest. Paul rner is the referee who knows the wrestling ropes.

South Africa press...

Being in South Africa was great. We were wrestling once a week, which meant there was a lot of free time. It was like a paid holiday. I was getting £100 a week - which worked out £100 a match - the hotels and food were paid for, and all we had to pay for was drink. Yes, we were doing a lot of drinking, but a bottle of beer cost half a rand, or 25p, and a bottle of 5-star brandy was the equivalent of £3.50, so drinking wasn't expensive. And everybody wanted to take us out, to pay for our drinks, to show us their country. We went up Table Mountain. We were taken to *braais*. We never went hungry.

The second time I went to South Africa - and yes, I'm getting ahead of myself here, but it shows how well we were always treated there - we did a show in Port Elizabeth. The guy who ran the show were a butcher, so when I get there he asks if I'd like something to eat. I say I would, and he comes back in with three burgers. They were each an inch thick, like a steak chucked on a big cob. And there were three of them. There's no way I'd be able to wrestle after eating all those, so I tell him I'll have the one burger and eat another one after the match. *Oh,* he says, *I've got something planned for after.*

He gives the other two burgers to someone else. We do our match, have a shower and get changed, and the promoter takes us into this a room with a beautifully laid out table. On it there are steaks, two or three inches thick, perfectly cooked. You didn't have to cut them, they just fell apart, and there was as much as you could eat. It were fantastic. They looked after us really really well in South Africa. It were the same whenever you went abroad, to be honest. You were fed well, you were paid well, you were always looked after.

Anyway, back to this first trip to South Africa, and I've got two matches left. For the next one, they've brought in a big lad from America, Steve Ray, and a Canadian lad who'd been there a month before. They didn't want people to know the Canadian was back, so he had to get off the aeroplane in a mask. That's how *kay fabe* the whole thing was. If he went out - even if he went down to the beach - he had to wear this mask the whole time so that no-one knew who he was. The three of us are hanging out between shows, having a few beers, and Steve heads off with a lady of the night.

A couple of days later, he's worried. His dick is itching, he says. No, worse than that, it's burning. So I ring the promoter, Sammy, and he comes over. *Oh no,* he says, *this'll be all over the papers.* And he's nudging me. *I'll have to get my mate to look at you. I can't send you to a proper hospital...* He makes a call. A little while later, this bloke turns up, takes a look at Steve's dick, and says *Yeah. You've got a very bad case of clapterootus.*

I think *Clapterootus???*

Steve says the burning is driving him mad - bear in mind that there was nothing visibly wrong, no discharge or sores or rash - and he'd really like some tablets for it. The bloke shakes his head. *No,* he says. *What you've got to do is put your dick in some boiling water, or as hot as you can stand it, every three hours without fail. All week. If you miss, you've got to start again.*

I can't believe what I'm hearing. It's really hard to keep a straight face, but Steve's nodding and hanging on every word. Anything to stop the burning. He starts the three-hourly boiling water treatment. A day or so later, I'm in a restaurant with him and the Canadian, and Steve's three hours are almost up. He's getting fidgety, worried he'll miss his appointment with boiling water. I tell him not to worry. Then I turn to the waiter and ask him for a pot of boiling water and a glass. It arrives.

Here you go.
I can't do it here!
Don't be daft.
What?
No-one's going to see what you're doing.
But...
The tablecloth will hide it.

So there I am in a restaurant, with Steve whimpering at the other side of the table, with his dick in a glass of boiling water, and myself and the Canadian doing our best to keep our faces straight. Next time we see Sammy the promoter, Steve tells him *It ain't worked. I've been doing it for a week, like the bloke said, and it ain't worked.*

Sammy asks Steve to tell him exactly what it is he's been doing.

I've been getting a glass of boiling water...
A glass?
Yeah.

No wonder it hasn't worked.
Huh?
A glass will let the heat out.
It will?
You need a cup.
I do?
You've got to use a cup. It'll hold the heat.
A cup...
Do it again, for another week.
OK...

And as I was leaving South Africa, he were starting another week of dipping his dick in hot water. There wasn't even anything wrong with him, except in his head, but we'd wound him up so bad he was convinced he had a dose. I mean, when the bloke said *A dose of clapterootus* I thought he's got to twig this is a wind-up, but he didn't, bless him.

Meanwhile, we had the small matter of a match in Capetown where we were tagging together. Even though Steve had spent several days dipping his dick in hot water every three hours, he was still able to get in the ring, but I'm not sure how much use he was. You wouldn't be after all that, would you?

The match were in a stadium that could seat 78,000 people, and it were full. Me and Steve were on last, against Gil Singh (his ribs had recovered enough for him to wrestle) and Gama Singh in a cage match. The cage was built out of the metal mesh they put as a frame within concrete, and the bars are about half an inch thick. Oh, and by this time, I've got my handcuffs back.

We open the changing room door to walk to the ring, and the noise is incredible. Steve Ray says to me that I should go out first. I walk out, look round, and he isn't behind me. Where's he gone? I go back into the changing room, and he's on the phone to his mother, and taking his boots off.

I'm on with this mad Englishman, he's going to get me killed, blah blah blah...

I took his phone off him, chucked it to one side, dragged him to the door with one boot still undone, and shoved him out in front of me so he had to get to the ring. There were 78,000 people waiting. The heat and the noise and the atmosphere were amazing. I was buzzing.

I push Steve into the ring, then I get in. Gama gets in next, and while Gil's outside dancing around, showing off to the crowd, I handcuff the door shut. He can't get in, we're kicking the shit out of Gama, and the crowd are going crazy. In the end, Gil had to climb up the cage, over the top, and into the ring that way. The crowd are practically rioting by this point, but in the end Gil and Gama win and we all get out alive. Even Steve.

After that match, Gil flew back to the UK and we went on to Durban, where I'd be wrestling Gama. The Durban promoter says to me *I need you to get them going straight away. I need them up straight away.* You'd have thought by now word would have reached him that wasn't a problem, but anyway... I get in the ring first, calling Gama everything under the sun, saying he's too short to fight (because he wasn't very tall). The crowd are screaming and shouting, and then Gama gets in the ring wearing a cloak and a turban, like he did, and he stands in the middle of the ring, playing to the crowd. Like I said, he weren't very tall. So when he half-turned away from me, I saw my chance, and I walked over and hit his turban off his head.

The crowd hit the roof.

They were climbing into the ring, and I'm hitting them and throwing them back off. Then Gama piles in on me, and everything calms down a little bit while the crowd watch the two of us go at it. The atmosphere were red-hot, though. After the match, when we're back in the changing room, I says to the promoter *Was that all right, then?*

He looks at me and shakes his head. *I thought they were going to kill you. What you did was like ripping a cross up in church. God, you take some risks you do!!*

I knew I did. That was my job.

That was what I was paid to do.

with Stevie Ray on my first visit to South Africa...

and with Anaconda on my second

Holidays

That first time I went to South Africa, I had no idea what to expect. I found myself wrestling in front of seventy thousand people and being treated like a king, and I loved every minute of it. You might think that coming back to the UK and driving up the motorway after a long day at work to get in the ring in front of six or seven hundred people on a wet Wednesday night would be a bit of a comedown, but you'd be wrong.

I never ever found it hard to motivate myself, because I loved what I did. As far as I was concerned, getting in a ring and wrestling was my job, and it didn't matter where I was, I loved it. After that first visit to South Africa, I think my first match back here was in Blackpool. Me and Stacks against Shirley and young Steve Logan. And yes, the buzz wasn't quite the same as when seventy thousand people are screaming at you, but because the room were so much smaller it still bounced off the walls, and when they announced me as *Scrubber Daly, just back from South Africa!* it gave me a thrill, and it gave the crowd something to shout about. Wrestling were great, and I just loved it.

Everyone in wrestling knew that there was no money in it here, not really. The money was when you got abroad. There were never any grumblings about it, though. You grafted here, and hoped you'd reach a certain level and get your payday out in South Africa or

India or the Gulf, where someone you knew would be doing a few shows and getting their payday and when the promoter asked them *Is there anybody else we should know about?* they'd put your name forward. That's what you hoped. The first time I went to South Africa, it was because Gil Singh had put my name forward. The second time I went, Drew MacDonald was already in South Africa and he rang to ask if I fancied another trip out there.

When?
Fortnight's time.
Yep, I'll do it.

That was how it worked. I sorted out my money direct with the promoter, and off I went. I still had a day job, but I wasn't at the quarry any more. By now I had my own milk round - well, a milk round franchised off the Co-op - and that gave me the freedom to fit my work round the wrestling. I had a lad who worked with me, and if I was away he could drive the float, so he'd do the round and Marg would do the books, and I'd still be earning money from the round while I were abroad wrestling. Having a holiday, as Marg would say.

I'm not having a holiday, I'm working!

I always used to bring Marg something back from abroad - I had a ring made for her on that first trip to South Africa, and she's still got it now - and these gifts were my way of saying thank you and keeping her sweet.

Because she always backed me, in everything I done. All my trips abroad, she never moaned - even though it could be a lonely existence, being a wrestler's wife. She rolled up her sleeves and worked. She got on with things. The only thing she'd ever complain about were the lad winding her up while I were away, telling her he couldn't come in to do the round in the morning, so she lay awake all night wondering how she'd get the milk delivered, and then she'd hear the float trundle off down the road first thing. When I came back home I'd give her a gift, and give him a clip round the earhole *Pack it in!* And that'd sort things out till next time I went away again.

Wrestling took me everywhere. That first trip to South Africa was an eye-opener as to how things could be, and I wanted more. Some folk might say I was lucky how quickly it all happened - I'd only been wrestling just over a year when I flew out to Johannesburg with Gil Singh - but I knew my rise was down to working hard, being a natural villain, and always giving 100%. Promoters loved that, crowds loved that, and I loved that. That meant everyone was getting what they wanted, and that meant I was getting asked to wrestle everywhere.

The first time I went to the Gulf - and I've been there five times - I'd never known heat like it. Horrendous. The halls we wrestled in were air-conditioned, but as soon as you stepped outside the sweat poured off you. I was 28-29 stone by then, which is a lot of weight to walk round in that kind of heat, and part of what the promoters had us do to promote the shows was walk round town centres so people could see us and be interested enough to buy tickets to the shows. That got me down a bit, if I'm honest, but in fairness to the promoters, they looked after us. We weren't overworked. Generally, we'd do three matches in ten days, for about £100 a week.

As you got more experienced, the pay went up. When I went to India, I were on £100 a day, and wrestling just once a week. That's a sweet deal. We did squeeze in an extra show, though. That was at the specific request of a bloke who rang the promoter to ask if we'd do an extra show just for him. The money was right, so we said yes. And that's how I ended up wrestling in front of a man who was the biggest mango exporter in the world, and who enjoyed his wrestling.

This was all a long way from that first match in Brent.

with Boston Blackie in India...

no, we don't accept payment in mangoes...

Cyprus

Wrestling took me all over the UK and all round the world. I've been to the Middle East five times, South Africa three, to Germany, France, and India. I was flown out there because of who I was and the job I did. And they always looked after me. I was always put in good hotels, had good food to eat. I had to buy my own drinks, yes, but nine times out of ten you could ponce them off the punters, and while I was out in whichever country it was I'd be taking my week's holiday off work. This meant I was getting holiday pay *and* my wrestling pay on top, so what wasn't to like? The one constant was that wherever I went, whoever I was wrestling, I always gave 100% when I was in the ring.

There may have been one exception to this, and that was when eight of us went to wrestle in Cyprus.

We were out there because of a wrestler called Tony Kostas. He was from Cyprus, and he'd booked the shows and flown us over. We were treated brilliantly. Everything were paid for - hotels, the lot. There was just one problem: hardly anyone came to the shows. Tony had put the shows in football stadiums, with the ring in the middle of the pitch, and the punters - the ones who'd turned up - sat in the seats round the outside. They were miles away from the action. I don't suppose it was much fun for them. It certainly wasn't much fun for us.

Fair play to Tony for trying, but it just didn't work, even though all of us did everything we could to try and promote the shows. When Tony asked us to go into town before a show and cause a bit of a scene so the press picked up on the story, we said OK. We set it up that Marty Jones, Alan Kilby, John Elijah the Bearman, and the other lads where in a shop, and I walked by with Drew MacDonald. Words were said. There was pushing and shoving. Next thing, we've started fighting in the shop. It made the papers, but nobody really understood what had happened, or why, and it didn't put any more bums own seats either. Unfortunately.

We were abroad, the sun was shining, the weather was hot. We had more free time than we knew what to do with, and the whole trip started to feel like a holiday. The first day we got there set the tone. Drew MacDonald - who loved nothing more than lying in the sun topping his tan up - said to me *I've found this stuff. I've been told about this. It'll make you go black, like.* It was baby oil with iodine in. Drew shook it up and spread it on. I did the same. Big mistake. As soon as the sun hit me, it was like chip fat burning. I had to dive in the pool before I fried, but Drew stuck it out and lay there, getting toasted.

John Elijah the Bearman - who were booked as The Mad Russian - he spent so long out in the sun that first day and burned the top of his head so badly that the skin split. Now, Bearman were a lovely guy, trained every day, was strong as an ox, and not quite the full shilling. He knew everything there was to know about bears, which is why he was called the Bearman. You could ask him *any-thing* about bears, and he had the answer. He liked to do bear hugs, too. But he'd burned his head really badly, and somebody took him to the shops and got him a hat to protect his head from the sun. It looked just like a baby's bonnet, and he walked round wearing it for the rest of the stay. Mad? Possibly. Russian? I'm not so sure.

John didn't have much luck while we were in Cyprus. A couple of days after burning his head, he stubbed or sprained or broke his big toe. It went completely black and swelled up so badly he couldn't get his boot on. He had to wrestle, so they cut the toe out of his boot and he wrestled with this great big bandage sticking out the end. At least the punters were so far away they couldn't see it.

The trip slowly descended into chaos. One day the organisers sent a minibus to take us all to the show, wherever it was. I turned to Drew.

I can't sit in the back.
Really?
I get sick.
You do?
Yep.
Me too.
Oh.
I've got to go in the front.
I've got to go in the front.
We'll both go in the front, then.

The minibus turns up, and it's a Hiace. This is going to be snug. DrewMcDonald jumps in the front, I jump in after him, he slides across so I can shut the door and... there's no room for the driver. There's 30-odd stone of me, another 24 stone of Drew. The front seat is full. The driver looks at us. *Where can I sit?* Drew tells him to get in the back, says he'll drive. The bloke's not having that. He shouts at Drew, Drew shouts back, and in the end the driver throws the keys away and walks off. Then we all hang around till they can find another minibus they can send, because the keys to the first one are lying somewhere in the Cypriot countryside. We squeeze in that second minibus, and head off to wrestle in the middle of a football pitch in front of a handful of punters who are so far away they won't be able to see what's happening anyway.

We wrestled about four times a week while we were out in Cyprus, and we were out there a fortnight. We did eight matches altogether, and none of them had a crowd. After the first match, when we saw how far away the punters were, and realised we were wrestling in the middle of nowhere, we quietly and collectively stopped taking it seriously. What was the point?

We did one show where we'd been on the drink all day before the match. I were so pissed that Drew had to help me to the ring. Well, we helped each other, truth be told. The two of us got in the ring, went through the motions, and stumbled back out again. The punters were that far away they wouldn't have had a clue.

That's the only time I've ever got in the ring and given less than 100%. Thank you, Cyprus, for a wonderful fortnight. We had so much fun it was unreal. It's just a shame that nobody came.

Fame

I'd made it to the top of British wrestling in very short order. My date sheets were full, I was driving up and down the country every night to climb in the ring in front of audiences of hundreds - sometimes thousands - and with wrestling being on TV every weekend, sometimes that meant I was on TV as well. All of this brought with it a certain amount of fame, or recognition, or notoriety, and that could be both a blessing and a right royal pain.

A lot of the good stuff was obvious. I was a name, so that got me work abroad where the pay was better, and I was well looked after while I was there. Some of the less obvious good stuff warmed your heart - like when me and Marg bought a house in Hartshill. I'd be out working in the garden and the local kids would be gathered on the waste ground opposite, all excited, telling each other *That's the wrestler! That's that wrestler!* and daring each other to go and talk to me. Not long after I'd gone back in the house there'd be a knock on the door, Marg'd answer it, and the bravest of the kids would say *Can we have his autograph, please?*

I always had a stack of black and white photos in the house, so I'd go to the door, sign one of the photos for the kid, and hand it over. There'd be an excited *Thanks!* and the kid would race back up the front path waving the photo, shouting to his friends *He's signed mine! He's signed mine!* and next thing there'd be ten kids queuing up the path waiting for their photo with a signature from the wrestler on the TV. If I went out, wherever I was going, the kids used to follow me, and – to me – that were great. I loved all that.

I only did the signed photos for the kids, though. After a match, if I was having a pint and people came up for an autograph, I'd tell them *No, I don't do them. Go away.* And ninety-nine times out of a hundred, folk understood that and left me alone. And most of the time, if I went out – and tell you the truth I didn't go out that much when I was wrestling, because I didn't really have the time – people generally respected my privacy and left me alone. It was only in the winter months, when my date sheet wasn't quite so full and I'd have four or five matches a week, so I'd two days off, that I might go out for a pint or two. But even in winter I'd be working a full-time job as well as wrestling, and while a lot of my sleep was snatched in the back of a car on the way to or back from a show, sometimes you just need to stop and have some time to yourself. Get some proper sleep.

So when I did go out, I just wanted a bit of time to myself, a chance to enjoy the same things I'd always enjoyed. I hadn't changed. Even though I'd been on TV and people knew who I was, I hadn't changed at all. When I took up wrestling I had friends say to me *You'll change once you've been on the TV!* I told them

I won't change. But you will.

And some of them did. They were the ones that – if I went out anywhere with them – would want to say *I'm with Scrubber Daly!* and make a big deal of it so they looked more important. They'd want to introduce me to the world and its dog, and I didn't want that. At all. All I'd be after were to go out and have a quiet drink, and sometimes people didn't want to let me do that. One time, I had some friends over from Ireland and I took them up the club. I'd no sooner walked in than some bloke comes over.

Hello!
Hello.
You're Scrubber Daly!
I know.
Can I announce you're in here?
You can...
Great!
But you do that...
Yes?
And I'll be out the door quicker than you can say it.
Why?
Because I've come in for a quiet pint...
I see.
And a sit down.
Oh.
I don't want anybody pestering me...
Right.
Which they will if you announce it.
Gotcha.

Fair play to him, he did leave me alone, and I was able to stay and enjoy the evening. If people did come up and ask me something, I'd talk to them, of course, but I just wanted a quiet pint. Kids coming up and asking for an autograph I didn't mind - they're kids - but people bothering me when I was after a quiet drink, that was really annoying, because then I had to play the villain. That was what was expected.

Even now, when wrestling hasn't got anything like the profile it had back then, if I'm training wrestlers I tell them that as soon as they come through the door of the training room, they've got to become the character they'll be in the wrestling ring. You have to leave your own personality outside. Be what you're going to portray in the ring. If you're a blue-eye, portray that. If you're a villain, portray that. Because if you don't, it's not going to come naturally. If you're a heel or a villain, you can't be laughing and smiling all the time, because that is not your role. And that's now.

Back in the day, if people started bothering me when I was out for a drink, they wanted Scrubber Daly the villain, when what I wanted was to be Mac out for a quiet pint. Most times, like I say, folk respected that. Sometimes they didn't, and sometimes that got me down.

As for blokes coming up wanting a fight so they could do their street cred some good - and that did happen - well, they learned their lesson, didn't they? As I've already explained, I was taught as a kid to get the first punch in, and once I'd got the first one in the person on the receiving end generally weren't interested in a second.

Which meant I could get back to my pint.

with British Bulldog, in Kuwait

the gentle giant

Stacks

These were the glory days of British wrestling, no doubt about it. I worked with a huge number of wrestlers over these years, and there were a lot of nice guys along the way. But the true gentleman among them all was Stacks. Or Giant Haystacks, as you'd have known him. There were no airs and graces with him. You walked in to the dressing room and he made you feel instantly welcome. Why? Because Stacks was a nice guy, through and through. Yes, he was a heel - and he played up to that, of course - and he was a giant of a man, and that meant a lot of people thought he'd be a monster, but he weren't.

I can't remember where I did my first match with him, but I do remember walking into the dressing room and seeing him sitting there, and thinking *Bloody hell!* When you saw him on TV, it didn't do his size justice. He was absolutely huge. 6'11", 42 stone, mass of black hair, and a beard. He was the picture of a villain, but out of the ring he was a really nice guy. In the dressing rooms, some stars would have their own room, but Stacks always sat with the lads, never in a room on his own.

When we worked together, the two of us would be wrestling in a tag match - usually against Shirley - especially if the small guy in the tags was someone a little bigger than normal. Someone like, say, Tom Tyrone or young Steve Logan. They'd be smaller than Shirley, obviously, but bigger than the usual small guy in a tag team. Then me and Stacks would tag together against them. We didn't just tag against Daddy, though. One time, me, Stacks, and Rasputin were in a tag against Pat Roach, Alan Kilby, and (I think) Ali Shan. Another time it was us against Pat Roach and Kilby.

Stacks' weight made him stand out from everyone else. It also meant normal rules did not apply. If he went to the toilet in the venue before you did, you could guarantee the seat would be ripped off when you got there, just because he weighed so much. If the toilet cubicle was particularly small, he might decide it was easier to take a dump in the shower. You'd find out about that when you went to have a shower yourself, assess the situation and decide that tonight having a shower could wait. You'd have one when you got home.

One time he was on an aeroplane – I wasn't with him, but I heard about it from someone who was – and Stacks needed to go the toilet. You don't need to be a genius to work out there's no way a man his size is getting into a plane toilet.

Houston, we have a problem.

The cabin crew thought about it and came up with a solution that involved the galley area, Stacks, and one big aluminium meal tray. They pulled the curtain across to give him some privacy, and let him do what he needed to do. But one of the lads sneaked up and pulled the curtains back, and there he was squatting over this tray, taking a dump.

The papers were full of stories that Stacks was huge because of how much he ate. There'd be pictures of him stood there by a table laden with food, and a story or an article about him eating six loaves of bread, five black puddings, four tins of beans, three trays of eggs, two sides of pig and a partridge in a pear tree for his breakfast.

All that was garbage, it was just giving the papers and the punters the story they wanted to hear. Stacks didn't eat like that. He couldn't. He was just naturally a giant.

Here's an example of what I mean.

We'd been down to Chelmsford once, and after the show there were a kebab shop we always used to stop at on the way home, off J2 on the M25. We'd turn off there, go down the road about five miles, and there was the kebab shop. Stacks would wait in the car. I'd go in. I'd get him a small kebab, no salad on it, just onion and meat. For myself, I'd have two proper kebabs with everything on them. *Just give me the works.* I'd have devoured one of mine, and be halfway through my second, and Stacks would still be munching on his half a one. At this point he'd turn round to me - and this is a guy who was forty-two stone - he'd turn round to me and say in his deep, deep voice

You fat greedy bastard. You've just ate two of them and I can only eat half a one.

Most people wouldn't have dreamed of calling me a fat greedy bastard to my face. Stacks had a way of making it OK.

The only time I ever wrestled against him were down at Bristol at Colston Hall, not long after wrestling stopped being on the TV. I got a phone call from Brian Dixon

Could you come down to Bristol for me?
No, it's a night off.
I'll give you double wages.
Who am I on with?
I'll tell you when you get down here.
OK...
Nice and easy.
Double wages?
Yes.

I drive to Bristol, and top of the bill is Stacks against some American guy. So why am I here? I find Brian.

I'm here.
Good. You're on with Stacks.
You're joking.
No.
I were down here last month...
I know...
Tagging with him.
The Yank wouldn't go on with him...
I see...
Said he was too big.
Well, he is a size...
So I've sent him home.
Right.
Waste of money.
OK.
You're wrestling him instead.
Double money?
Double money.

Now, Stacks is the biggest villain of all, so to my mind it stands to reason that when the two of us get in the ring, everyone's going to be cheering for me, because I'm the blue eye going toe-to-toe with Stacks. Did they hell. I went out - nothing. Stacks comes out and they all went crazy, cheering him, shouting encouragement.

We wrestled. Now, if you're going to beat someone like Stacks, you've got to play a bit fast and loose with the rules, that's the way I see it. Before a match, I'd enter the arena with a horseshoe hanging round my neck. It was part of my costume. Then when I got in the ring, I'd give it to my manager to look after. On this particular night, Pete Lapaque was my manager. I've got Stacks in the corner, giving him some stick, and I get Pete to pass me the horseshoe. And I hit Stacks on the head with it. Twice. There's blood pouring down his face, and he's chuntering away. He does not look happy.

Luckily for me, the referee disqualifies me. I get out the ring and say to Pete *I think we'd better fuck off before Stacks comes back.* We get our money, hop in the car, and we're gone. We left Bristol so fast we had to stop at a services on the M5 to get changed.

I didn't see Stacks till a few days later. We were wrestling together somewhere and he walks in the dressing room and says *You fucking twat. If you're hitting someone with a horseshoe, don't hit them that fucking hard.* He had about eighteen stitches in his head, but he laughed about it. Hitting him with the horseshoe had got some good heat, it got the crowd wild, and we both knew that's what wrestling were all about. It were no surprise that Stacks were fine about it. And it wasn't a surprise that I weren't going to take the risk of finding out whether he were fine about it on the night, when there were blood pouring down his face and he were seeing stars.

Oh no. Pete and me were back in the changing rooms, grabbing our stuff and we were gone. You can only push a gentleman so far.

would you hit this man with a horseshoe?

Weight

I'd always been a big lad. I'd been brought up to clear my plate - you ate everything in front of you or you couldn't go out to play. If you didn't eat your dinner, you couldn't watch the telly. So you never left anything. It were as simple as that, because your mum and dad had to work hard to get the money to put the food on the table, and the experience of rationing was still fresh in their memory, so the idea you wouldn't eat what was in front of you was unthinkable. Your dinner was put down in front of you and there was no *I don't want this, can I have that, and what about the other?* No. You can't. That's what you've got. There's your dinner. Get on with it. And that's how I were brought up.

It weren't anything fancy - all vegetables, and potatoes, and a bit of meat - but there was nothing I didn't eat. Not when I was at home, anyway. Puddings at school were something else - some of them were vile. I didn't like tapioca, semolina, or anything that looked like frogspawn. If I was at home though, and mum made a rice pudding or apple pie, or used the old bread to make bread and butter pudding, well, I loved it. It were only at school I had things I didn't like. I'd tried them all, but some of them were so grim - like the custard at junior school - that I didn't ever want to eat them again.

So I were always a big lad. When I was playing football, and when I started training with Pat Roach, I weighed about twenty-two stone. That was pretty big -

Shirley only weighed twenty-five - but when I went to that meeting with Max Crabtree in Digbeth he said *I need you to put some weight on, kid, and grow a beard. We can use you then.* I grew the beard more or less straight away. It takes weeks to grow, doesn't it? The weight took a little longer.

I'd say that by the end of my first twelve months in wrestling, my weight had crept up to twenty-six or twenty-seven stone. You might think that I'd had to work really hard to put on an extra five or six stone, but I hadn't. I wasn't deliberately eating more, and I wasn't eating anything different from what I had before, either. It was purely down to the lifestyle. I couldn't eat before a match - if I did, taking the bumps would make me sick as a dog - and by the end of an evening when it was all done and dusted and everyone had gone home, the only things you could get were fish and chips, or a chinese, or kebabs, and I'd be eating those seven nights a week, then sitting in a car for two or three hours, and not burning it off. I'd drive home, get into bed, fall asleep, get up for work in the morning, and do the same thing again. All those extra calories had to go somewhere, and they turned up as weight.

The main effect of that first few stone in my first year of wrestling was that I felt stronger. I could pick somebody up and chuck them about without blinking an eye. I could use the weight. It gave me an advantage, I must admit, but it didn't hinder me in any way. I was wrestling and working and eating, and getting bigger. It didn't change the way I wrestled, or what I could do at work.

There was never a problem with that, and my weight never bothered me. Being bigger was part of the job. It was my image. Part of the reason I got offered wrestling matches abroad was because I was so big, so what wasn't to like? The extra weight and the extra bulk just made me feel stronger.

Looking back, it's obvious that I wasn't eating properly, or at the right times. I was eating junk food seven nights a week, basically, and that's going to make anyone put weight on. With me, even more so. Before I'd ever started wrestling, I'd gone into hospital and been kept on a strict calorie-controlled diet to find out why I didn't lose weight even though I was working full-time and playing football every moment I could. They kept me in for a week and allowed me 200 calories a day, which meant I ate a lot of salads. I'd have a boiled egg in the morning (77 calories there) and salad for the rest of the day. No meat. As many pickles as I wanted, because the vinegar was supposed to help break down fat.

The weight should have dropped off me. It didn't. They even checked Marg's bag when she came to visit, to make sure she wasn't sneaking in anything I shouldn't have. She wasn't.

At the end of that week - one week of eating boiled eggs - they found out that my metabolism preferred turning food into fat to turning it into energy. I'd always been big, and I always would be big. I'd put on weight if I had an ordinary 9-5. Wrestling, and eating late at night, helped put the weight on quicker. Or didn't help, depending how you look at it.

By now, when I was in the ring I was wrestling in my trademark dungarees. I'd started off in a black leotard, black trunks, and boots, but I didn't wear them for long. The dungarees were Lucky Gordon's idea. So were the horseshoe, and the chain. No-one else had done that, and it became an integral part of my image, wherever I was in the world.

Professionally, I was in my prime. All the time, my weight kept creeping up. It stayed at twenty-six stone for a while, then started going up again.

I reckon my weight reached its peak in about 1988-90, when I weighed thirty-six stone. I was working driving lorries by then, and working hard, so I should have been burning the weight off. It wasn't as if I spent my day just sitting in the cab, backing a lorry into a bay, and having someone sign the paperwork and send me on my way. I was climbing in and out of the cab, climbing up on top of the load to put the sheet on and strap it all down, I was in and out the lorry all the while. My weight didn't stop me doing any of that, but however active I was it still didn't make any difference.

I was forty years old, I weighed thirty-six stone, and my knees had started to notice. They were killing me. In 1995, I went to the doctors. They sent me for an X-ray, looked at the results and told me the news.

I needed two new knees.

There was no gristle in my knee joints - my weight had worn it away - and now my knees were just bone rubbing against bone. They wouldn't give me replacement knees, either.

You can have them when you're sixty.
Sixty?
Yes?
I want them now!
No, Mr Hardiman.
Why?
Your weight.

They told me replacement knees will normally last about ten years. Then the replacements need replacing. When those need replacing - and they could only do the operation three times in total - I'd end up with two stiff legs I'd never be able to bend. I was forty. With my weight, I'd be lucky to get five years out of replacement knees, maybe three years for the second set. If they operated now, like I wanted them to, I'd be immobile by the time I was fifty.

What was there to do? Nothing.

I kept working.
I kept wrestling.
And I put up with the pain.

The End

I'd started being a wrestler just as British wrestling had its last days of glory. From that first match in Brent, I got to the top of the tree and was tagging with Stacks in less than twelve months. 1985, and I was top of the bill. I wanted to be on television - everyone who wrestled wanted to get on television - and to get on television you had to work for Dale Martins, so that's what I did.

I can't imagine having done anything better with my life. The hours were long, the pay was poor, but I loved every minute of it. There were so many good times. Like the night we were at Cheltenham Town Hall, and as we rushed out in a hurry - we hadn't even got changed, just grabbed our bags, got in the car, and left as fast as we could - the police were rushing in. It was kicking off, and we were the ones who'd kicked it. That was how it was, and I hope the stories in this book have given you an idea of what that time were like. But it was all about to change.

In 1985, ITV brought *World of Sport* to a close. It had been running for twenty years, and helped make household names out of a string of wrestlers, but ITV bosses felt it was time things moved on. They still showed wrestling for a few years, in a new lunchtime slot, but that petered out in 1988. Without that TV coverage, maintaining wrestling's profile was going to be next to impossible, however hard Max tried. Television had given wrestling a presence in everyone's living rooms, and now that access had gone.

I stopped working for Max in 1994, just before he packed it in for good. I'd got a new job, and the chap I was driving for now wouldn't let me have time off to go haring up and down the country to be a wrestler, then turn up at work having had next to no sleep.

I could see his point. So for the next few years I worked for a local promoter, Jake, who were based in the Tamworth area. This meant I could do my day's work on the lorries, get cleaned up and get changed, do his shows in the evening, and get my kip in. They were local shows, but Jake was paying me £50 a show, so he'd doubled my money. I'd work the local shows for him, and save my holidays, and then once a year a van load of us would head up to Scotland for a week to to a string of shows for Jake there.

The lads who worked for Jake were a great bunch. We'd stop in a bed and breakfast for that week, and during the day we'd go bowling or play mini golf, or whatever. We'd have a laugh, and we'd work hard. There wasn't anybody else turning up to put the ring up - those days were gone - that was part of our job now. My knees were so bad by then that there was no way I could muck in with putting the ring up, so I pulled my weight by driving the minibus all week. We worked together. We were a team.

What we did had changed. It had to. Some folk who came along knew me as Scrubber, but now a lot of the folk who were paying their money to come to a show had only seen WWE on the TV. They wanted American wrestling, so that's what we gave them. I became 'UK Earthquake', because the Americans had got an Earthquake. We had an 'Undertaker'. It worked. A lot of the time, the houses were full. These were still good times.

My knees were shot and I weighed way too much to be healthy, but I still loved getting in the ring. I couldn't imagine ever stopping - and maybe I'd have died in the ring with my boots on like Mal Kirk - but then Jake decided he was going to stop promoting shows. Suddenly the decision was made for me.

I wasn't going to be a wrestler any more.

I settled into driving lorries, and about twelve months after my last show for Jake I shaved off my beard. I'd only grown it because Max had told me to. *Grow a beard, you're too baby-faced to be a villain.* And now I didn't need to be a villain any more. Was shaving my beard off some kind of statement? Was I drawing a line under my life as a wrestler? Not really. I just went upstairs, looked in the mirror and thought *I'm going to shave this off.* And I did. No particular reason. Marg didn't even notice for an hour or so.

What I looked like without a beard was... kind of odd. Every time I caught sight of the clean-shaven me it came as a shock. Still, in for a penny in for a pound. I decided to get my hair cut as well. I had that mullet at the time, lovely red hair, really long down the back. It had been a nightmare to keep clean back when I was working at the quarry, when I'd have to wash it every day to get the dirt and the dust out. That was all in the past now. I went into the barbers, sat in the chair, and said

I want about a half-inch.
Taking off?
No, leaving on.
Are you sure?
Yes, half an inch.

He took a deep breath, picked up the scissors, and made the first cut. By the time I walked out of there I looked totally different. Marg might not have noticed I'd shaved, but she noticed the haircut.

It was time to start looking after myself.

That meant it was time for the gastric band.

Gastric Band

Those last few years, when I were wrestling for Jake, the pain from my knees was incredible. I'd get in the ring and the sweat would just pour out of me, purely because of the pain of bone grinding on bone. They needed replacing, but I couldn't get them done till I lost some weight. A lot of weight. And I knew for a fact the only way I was going to lose that weight was if I got fitted with a gastric band.

I'd always been big, you see, even when I was young and playing football every hour I could. I'd always liked food, too, and however much I ate, I never felt full. Where Stacks was a giant of a man who didn't eat much, I was a big man who'd clear his plate. It was part of who I was.

To give you an idea of how much I could eat in the normal run of things, there was a pub not far from us which did a meal with a 2lb steak. I'd eat it - no problem - with onion rings, chips, salad, and peas. I'd have had a starter, of course, and a couple of beers, and I'd have a sweet after.

There was another place I'd go to over Coventry way, which offered what they called a 'mammoth' mixed grill. It came out on a huge metal platter, and the platter was full, laden with food. There'd be a 16oz steak, a big piece of gammon, three sausages, black pudding, burgers, liver, pork chop, lamb chop, kidneys, two eggs, everything.

Then there'd be a mountain of chips on a separate plate. Most people wouldn't come close to eating all that. I'd eat every last mouthful.

It was a lot of food, but I never felt full. I could eat all that, and although I wouldn't order another, I wouldn't feel full in myself. You know how people can have a meal and think *Oooh, I couldn't eat another thing!* I'd never felt like that, ever, and that meant the weight had piled on. Losing it was going to need something drastic.

I applied for a gastric band. It took two and a half years of fighting my corner to get it. The first doctor they sent me to in Birmingham said he wouldn't fit me with a gastric band because my BMI was too high. I thought that made me *exactly* the kind of person who should have a gastric band fitted, but he wasn't having it.

It won't work on you.
How do you know?
You weigh too much.
How do you know?
We've weighed you.
You haven't.
We have.
The scales aren't working.
Oh.
So you haven't weighed me.
Well, it still won't work.
How do you know.
Because I do.
But –
I'm a surgeon.

Instead, he offered me a stomach bypass. This does exactly what it says on the tin - they cut your digestive tract above your stomach, and again below the stomach, and sew the two ends together, bypassing the stomach completely. After that, food just goes straight through you. The doctor warned me I might never work again, and I wouldn't be able to drive, because I'd always need to be near a toilet. It sounded barbaric.

I told him I wasn't having it, he told me I still wasn't getting a gastric band, and I went home, miserable and angry. It was always the same. Whatever was wrong with me, a doctor would tell me it was down to my weight. If I had a boil on my foot, it'd be my weight. If I couldn't get a gastric band, it was because of my weight. If I was miserable and angry, my weight would be to blame.

A week later, his secretary rang to see if I'd changed my mind. I hadn't. There was no way I was having that stomach bypass. Anything was better than that.

If the doctor in Birmingham wouldn't fit a gastric band, we'd find someone else who would. Marg had read an article in a magazine about a woman called Sharon Bates - who was the first lady to have a band fitted, over in France - and who was now offering it in the UK. It were private, but if the NHS wouldn't help me, maybe these people would. On a sunny Saturday morning, we drove down to Bristol to meet them.

I had a good chat with Sharon and the doctor there, and they were really helpful, but the operation was going to cost in the region of £7500. Getting that kind of money together wasn't going to be easy, but what choice did I have? We'd have to find a way of doing it.

Then the secretary rang again to ask why I wouldn't have the bypass. The conversation went much as it had the time before. *No, you haven't weighed me... Yes, I have been to a psychologist... Yes, I did try a stay in hospital on a controlled diet... No, it didn't work....*

I'd explored the options that were open to me, and I believed a gastric band was my best chance of losing the weight I needed to lose. I just wanted the opportunity.

The to-ing and fro-ing over this went on for months. The secretary would ring to relay me their position, and I'd answer the phone and tell them my view hadn't changed. If Marg answered the phone she'd tell them the same. Eventually, after nearly two years of phone calls, they agreed the Bristol team could fit my gastric band and it would be paid for by the NHS. It was the news I'd been waiting to hear.

I picked up the phone and rang Bristol.

The doctor in Bristol - Andrew, his name was - asks me to go down there to talk through what they'll do. First I had to stand astride two sets of scales so they could weigh me, because one set wouldn't handle my bulk, and confirm I weighed thirty-six stone. How much of that did I think I could lose to help with the operation? I told him. He nodded, and said that would be a start, but the tablets he was going to prescribe me would help.

He told me what they were called, and I shook my head. I'd had these before. *Let me guess,* says Andrew, *you were shitting through the eye of a needle, right?* Right. That was exactly what happened. I'd taken these tablets and had to carry a bag of clothing round with me at work, because - and there's no nice way to put this - oil would just leak out of me.

Andrew promised that if I followed his instructions, there'd be no problems this time round. I still wasn't keen, because of what had happened last time, but Marg persuaded me to give it a go. She was right. I'd fought so hard to get to this point, I might as well do what they said.

I took a deep breath, and agreed to the tablets. I was given a list of things I couldn't eat while I was taking them, and two or three times a week I'd get a phone call to check how I was doing. The result? No problems at all, and - every bit as satisfyingly - I lost twice as much weight as they wanted me to.

The tablets had been important to show that I'd got my head round the idea of losing weight, and to make it clear to the medical team that I was serious about changing how I did things. Now, I could see a light at the end of the tunnel, I could begin to believe that I wasn't going to weigh thirty-six stone forever. Next came the yogurt diet. For two weeks, I could eat as many yogurts as you like in a day - fruit ones, any flavour I liked - but that was all. I couldn't eat anything other than yogurt.

What's that do?
It shrinks your liver.
Oh.
When we fit the gastric band...
Yeah?

It's a keyhole operation.
OK.
We have to move your liver.
I see.
If the liver's big and floppy it can tear...
Right.
And then we've got to open you up properly.

I didn't like the sound of that, so I started the yogurt diet. I thought it would be hard, but it weren't, because - like I say - I could see light at the end of the tunnel. I had a goal, and if that meant I was eating nothing but yogurt for fourteen days, that was fine. I was one week into my fortnight of yogurt, and the phone rang. Bristol had a cancellation.

Can you come down Tuesday and we'll do it?

That next Tuesday, my mate Paul and his missus Rosemary drove me and Marg down to the hospital in Bristol. I was taken to a little room where they weighed me, and discovered that since I first started preparing for the operation and taking the tablets I'd lost nearly ten stone. Ten stone lost before I'd even had the gastric band!

Andrew offered me the option of forgetting about the band and stopping on the tablets, said some people chose to do that, but I said I still wanted the gastric band.

The door's open, and we're having a laugh, and someone wheels a defibrillator down the corridor and leaves it outside my room. Paul points at it.

'Kinell!
What?
That ain't a good sign, is it?
What??
Putting that outside your room.
What???
The defibrillator!I
Shut up!
But...
You're bad news you are!

We're laughing and joking, and then the staff let me know it's time for me to go down to theatre. They tell Marg the procedure will take about two hours, so she heads off to Bristol with Paul and Rosemary to grab a bite to eat. They come back later, expecting me to be out of theatre. I'm not. Three hours go by. Four hours go by. Five hours pass, and Marg is crawling up the walls. By the time Sharon appears, she's beside herself. *Where is he? I'm going to go and find him! If I have to go in every room, I'll go in every room!*

Sharon tells her I'm in recovery, and that I'm all right.
Now.

Apparently, the operation went fine. I was in recovery, and all of a sudden my heart just stopped. That defibrillator Paul had been joking about? They had to use it to jump start me. They wheeled me up in a bed to see them all and Paul didn't know what to say, bless him. You can imagine how awkward he felt about it all, but as far as I could see it was just one of them things. The doctors didn't know why it happened, but the old joke about the operation being a success and the patient dying very nearly came true. I lay in recovery and *Boom.* My heart stopped. Luckily they managed to get me going again, and I'm here to tell the tale.

Normally the hospital let folk go home on the day of their operation, but after what had happened to me I had to stop overnight. When I woke up the next morning, there were a bloke sitting at the side of my bed. *Don't panic,* he says. *I were on the team yesterday, and I thought I'd come and see how you were getting on.* I told him I were feeling fine, that I were looking forward to going home. *Good,* he says. He stands up to leave, pauses for a moment, and tells me

It was touch and go, you know. I don't think you know how close it was.

I lay there in the bed, with his words going round my head. Getting the gastric band fitted had nearly killed me. Maybe the doctor in Birmingham had a point, and maybe he didn't. The band was fitted now.

We'd see what happened next.

New Me

Paul, Rosemary, and Marg came back down to Bristol to pick me up. On the way back home we stopped at a services because I needed the toilet, and I began to learn just how much my life was going to change. All I could take for the next three weeks was fluid, no solid food at all, and all I could manage to get down me at those services were half a cup of tea. That was something new.

After three weeks of fluids, I was allowed to move on to soup. A little while after that, I could add mashed potato to the list of things I could eat. Once I'd mastered that, I was allowed to eat anything mushy. Finally, I was allowed to start eating little bits of solid food, and I mean little bits. This was me, the man who could polish off a whole 'mammoth' mixed grill, who'd have the biggest steak on the menu when he went out, and finish everybody else's like as not, but I was learning those days had gone forever. At first, it were hard. I'd think about all the things I'd love to be eating, but couldn't eat any more.

Before I'd had the band fitted, I'd thought the thing I'd miss most would be meat, because if I hadn't got a chunk of meat on my plate then I hadn't got a dinner. What I actually missed, strangely enough, was the cheese and onion french stick I'd buy from a batch van at the side of the road when I was working on the lorries. I really loved those french sticks. But now I couldn't have them, and that was what I missed more than anything.

The french stick was out because I couldn't eat bread anymore. It was one of the foods I had to avoid because bread would swell and block my new restricted gut. I couldn't have fizzy drinks either, because the gas could build up in my stomach and lift the gastric band. Both of those were out, and I'm not going to say it wasn't difficult, because it was. There were times when it was very very difficult, because I'd always loved my food.

After a short while I learned what I could eat and what I couldn't eat, because if I got it wrong I'd be violently sick. I'd be violently sick if I ate too much, and I'd be violently sick if I ate something my body didn't like me having. If I ate meat, I had to chew it and chew it and chew it - they call the gastric band the chew-chew diet, because you've got to chew your food so much. The band forces your stomach into the shape of an egg timer, and anything you swallow that's too big gets stuck. Normally, you'd just have a drink and wash the food through, but that doesn't work when you've got a gastric band. Once something's stuck, anything you eat will just hit it and come straight back up.

I've been sick for three or four hours sometimes, trying to get something back top that's stuck. I've even laid with my feet in the air to try and get it back. Once, I got a piece of pineapple stuck, and I couldn't move it whatever I tried. It was there for three days and I still couldn't move it. I couldn't eat anything, I couldn't drink anything. I rang the people in Bristol for advice, and they said I'd have to go there so they could check it out. I drove down, they put me on the X-ray machine, and saw that the piece of pineapple was stuck right in the band.

The solution to this problem was simple: I've a port in my left side, a round metal port, so that at any point they can either pump fluid in to fill the band up, or take fluid out to let it down. When you first have the band fitted, it's set to reduce your stomach to a size where you'll be losing weight. Once you get to your target weight, they take a little bit of the fluid out, so you can eat a little bit more and your weight stays constant. Taking fluid out of the band now let it down, the pineapple passed through, they pumped the fluid back in and I drove back home.

Going through the different stages of what I could eat - fluids, soups, soft food, then solids - took a good six months. The first time me and Marg went out somewhere and I could eat properly, I had a little bowl of shepherds' pie - and I could only eat a quarter of it. I said to Marg

There's something funny here.
What?
Something's not right.
What do you mean?
I can't get any more down.
Well, you're full.
Full?
Yes, full.
I don't understand.
Well, your stomach's like an egg timer now.
Yes...
The top bit's full. You've got to wait...
Wait?
Wait, before you can have anything else.

I can't tell you how hard it was to get my head round this sensation of being full, because it was something I'd never known before. Like I say, the gastric band changed everything in my life, so there was a huge amount to learn, and to adjust to. To help with this, we had meetings every six months or so, down in Bristol. All the people who had gastric bands would get together and talk.

You'd hear how other people were doing, share your experiences, get some support, and give some support where you could, too. In these meetings I learned that losing weight isn't a constant, smooth trajectory – there'll be times when you're losing weight, and times when you're losing inches – and that by measuring myself I'd learn to tell when I was losing pounds and when I wasn't, and accept that sometimes my weight loss would plateau out as my body shape changed, and that then, suddenly, the pounds would start dropping off again.

I also learned we couldn't all eat the same things. Even now, there are some things I can't eat. Chips are one. You know when someone has fish and chips and you smell them and it smells like the best thing ever and you nick one off the plate? If I do that I can guarantee you within ten minutes I'll be upstairs in the toilet being sick as a dog. Yet I can go to the chip shop and have a scallop – or potato fritter, or klondike, or whatever you call them where you live – and it's not a problem. I can eat them, but I can't ever do chips.

I can eat fish if it's fresh, but not if it isn't. I can only eat meat if it's mince. If I nick a bit of meat off the chicken legs I do for the dogs' dinners, ten minutes later I'll be sick. It's just the way it is.

All this was hard. I won't pretend it wasn't. It still is hard, sometimes. But I had a goal - which was to lose weight - and it worked. Once I had the band fitted I lost about half a stone a month, so by the time I went out for that shepherds' pie with Marg, I'd already lost about three stone, and that was on top of the ten stone I'd lost before the band was fitted.

I felt better when I was walking about. I weren't out of breath so much. The pain in my knees eased up. I was getting better and better in myself, and that meant I got less bothered about what I could and couldn't eat, because I was seeing and feeling the benefits of what I was doing.

Now, there's no fluid in my band. It's been there that long that my stomach's shrunk, so I can't hardly eat anything, and I've re-educated myself about how much is enough. There was a time when nothing was enough, when I could devour a mammoth grill and still not feel full, but those days are gone.

Now, one of my favourite meals will be a bowl of grated cheese, onion, a tin of tuna, and some mayonnaise, all mixed up together. Maybe with a boiled egg in there, so it's a meal packed with protein. I eat it and feel great. Marg says it looks like a bowl of sick, but I love it. I could eat that every night. Yes, there are times when I see a programme on the telly where they're cooking a chunk of steak or whatever, and think how much I'd love a big juicy steak myself, but as Marg always reminds me, I wouldn't be alive if I hadn't had the gastric band.

And she's right.

The band gave me my life back. I'm sixty-six now, and you can't carry thirty-six stone around when you're sixty-six years old. My heart would have give way years ago - I was struggling when I was forty, truth be told - and if I hadn't had the band I wouldn't still be here. And I do like being here. It's as simple as that.

Skin

The band did its job. I lost sixteen stone in total, and that's a lot of weight. I was moving around more easily, and I felt better in myself, but whatever I did now I was doing it in the skin of a man who was twice my size. When you put on a lot of weight, your skin stretches to accommodate the extra bulk. When you lose that weight, you're a smaller person in a suit of loose skin, and in my case the weight loss left me with folds of loose skin all over - where my belly had been I had what they call an apron of skin that hung down to my knees. I used to have to tuck it in to my trousers.

This wasn't pleasant, but it wasn't a surprise either. Before I'd ever got the gastric band fitted, I got the hospital to agree that once I'd lost the weight, the NHS would fund the skin removal when the time came. If you have to pay for it yourself, it's going to cost over £20,000 and we didn't have that kind of money. They promised to fund the operations.

When we went back to them so we could book those operations, they changed their minds. They told me they hadn't got the funding. I said I'd done everything they asked and *Look how much weight I've lost!*

I reminded them they'd promised to pay for it, but they kept saying no. Just as I'd had to fight for the gastric band, I had to fight and fight again for them to pay for these operations. Finally, thankfully, they said they'd cover the cost. I was put in touch with a surgeon who worked down in Plymouth. That might seem a long way to go - there's hospitals nearer Nuneaton, after all, - but I'd been warned to be very careful about who did these operations, because you really don't want them going wrong. The surgeon had an office in Cheltenham, so I drove down there and he examined me. He looked at my apron. *Yes,* he said, *I'll have to cut you round the middle, cut you round again, take the middle bit out and sew you back together.*

He made it sound so easy.

The operation lasted thirteen hours. I drove down to Plymouth, they put me under, he cut me all round like a tyre, then sewed me up. They recycled some of the fat they'd cut off me and used it to rebuild my backside. *You won't have a backside like Beyonce, but you will have one.*

I was in hospital in Plymouth for just over a week. When I first came round from the op, I had four drains on each side of me, so blood and fluid and gunge could drain out. They'd given me a morphine pump too, but I didn't use it - there was pain, but it was a middling level of pain, a 5/10 level of pain, so I stuck with paracetamol. The doctors monitored how much fluid was passing through the drains, and as the levels dropped, they'd remove them. After a week, I was down to just two.

I'd gone down to Plymouth with Marg, and we'd hired a log cabin for her and the dog to stay in, and every day she'd come in to see me. When I was down to just the two drains they let me out to stay at the cabin. That way, if there were any problems, the hospital was close to hand. I stayed at the log cabin for two or three days, and then they said I could go home and get the last two drains taken out at hospital back in Nuneaton. We drove back up from Plymouth with me holding a Tesco carrier bag. In the bag was a pouch, and whatever came out of the drains went into the pouch.

This was my new accessory. When we stopped at the motorway services to stretch our legs and have a cuppa, the Tesco bag came with me, and it stayed with me till the drains had done their work and Nuneaton hospital took them out. That felt really weird, because the pipes had been laid in all the way long the incision, so each one were about a foot long. They cut the stitch that held the pipe in and as they pulled it out I could feel it moving inside me. Very odd.

Overall, it took me just over a month to heal, I reckon. A nurse would visit regularly to check the wounds stayed clean and didn't get infected, and check how I felt. How did I feel? I felt a lot better. I felt better in myself, and I felt better when I looked in the mirror. Once I was completely healed, it was time to take the staples out.

I don't know exactly how many staples there were - I didn't count - but they tell me it was something like 250. That's a lot of staples. I stood in the middle of the treatment room as they pulled them out, one after the other, with a pair of pliers. They got halfway round me and I flaked out. I remember saying *I'm going...* and that were it.

Bang. I were gone.

I'd lost a lot of weight, but there was still a fair bit of me when I came crashing down on the floor. It wasn't the pain that made me pass out, I think it was just standing there so long while they pulled staple after staple out of me. So what they did then was take every other one all the way round, and came back the next day and took the rest out.

This was just operation number one. There were five more to come. In all, I'd have six operations over the next four years. Getting all this loose skin cut away weren't an easy process. Make no bones about it.

The second operation was six months after the first. In this one, they sliced me from the bottom of my breastbone straight down past my belly button, and got rid of the loose skin at my sides. Again, I didn't need the morphine pump, even when the wound got infected and a big yellow blob came up just beneath my ribs and needed draining off.

In operation three, they cut away all the loose skin on the inside of my legs. That was OK. Next came operation four, and it was the worst one by far.

In this one, they made an incision up the inside of one arm from the elbow, all the way across my chest - going round the nipples, because they need to stay where they are and they need to be kept alive - and down the other arm to the elbow. When I came round after that one, the pain were horrendous. They'd warned me that they'd be cutting skin away from a lot of nerves and muscle, and that it wouldn't be a comfortable experience.

They were right.

I was straight on the morphine pump, the pain were that bad. It hurt. It really hurt. But the weirdest thing about it was when I was coming round after the op.

It was 2 o'clock in the morning, and I was still a bit dozy - partly because of having had an op and partly because it's 2 o'clock in the morning - but I was sure I could feel something happening, something unexpected. I open my eyes, and there's a nurse rubbing my nipples. They've put gauze dressings over my nipples to keep them warm while I recover, and she's lifted the dressings away and is rubbing them with her finger. *It's OK,* she says, *I'm only checking they're still warm and alive. And pink.*

Blimey. All this on the NHS! I thought. And I went back to sleep.

I know for a fact they stapled my chest back together with 250 staples in that operation, and when I'd healed and the nurse removed them, I felt every last one of them come out. There were so many staples that it took three appointments to get the job done. In the first one, she took out every third staple; when I went back, she did every other one of what was left; the third time, she finished it off. It would have been quicker to have weighed me in for scrap.

I had two further operations. One where they took my belly button, and another where they took away yet more skin from my stomach because I'd lost more weight and the skin was hanging again. I got used to drains coming out of me, and pigtails, and pouches of fluid, and staples, and nurses with pliers, and everything that went with having all my loose skin cut away. I spent so much time in the Plymouth hospital that the staff all knew me. They knew I'd been a wrestler, and they knew they could have a laugh with me. Even the surgeon enjoyed a bit of banter with me when he came round to see me as I was recovering in bed.

Mr Hardiman...
Yes?
You were a wrestler?
I was.
Hmmm.
Why?
I was watching a video of you...
You were?
While I cut you open.
Er...
Very interesting.
Thanks.
Don't worry, I kept my concentration.
Good.
Mostly.
What?
Goodbye, Mr Hardiman!

Was I still Scrubber Daly? I wasn't sure. It had been years since I'd been in the ring. I'd retired well before I had the band fitted, then there'd been a couple of years of losing weight, and after that getting all these operations done took still more time. The second op was six months after the first, and then - because six months wasn't proving long enough for me to heal properly - they were every twelve months, so you can see how long it all took.

That might sound like a bad thing, but it wasn't, because every time I went under the knife, I'd be off work for about eight weeks. I was driving machines at the tip then, and even though I'd save my holiday up, I hadn't got enough holiday to cover all that time off. I'd have four weeks on sick pay - at £68 a week - and four weeks on holiday pay, and we had to find the money for the cabin down in Plymouth as well, so having an operation once a year helped ease the financial pain.

We struggled, I'll be honest, but we got through. We got through it all and we were OK. I could see change - change for the better - after each of the operations, and that kept me going even when things were hard. Marg were a strong character too, she always has been strong, but it was hard for her too. After each operation, she'd be there for me while I were recovering, but as soon as we got home and she knew she could relax, that was when it affected her. She'd have upset stomach and all sorts.

These years where I had the band fitted and commuted down to Plymouth to have bits of me cut away put a strain on us both, even if we didn't know it at the time.

Crushed

By now it was 2013, I think, and I'd turned my life around. My heart and my lungs and my knees and just about every part of me weren't dragging thirty-six stone around every minute of the day, thanks to the gastric band; I weighed nearly half of what I had done; I'd had the masses of loose, hanging skin cut away; and I was healthier than I'd been in years.

I felt great. I started making plans to do things I wanted to do. I'd always fancied having a boat and going sea fishing, so Marg and I talked about the two of us running a little hotel, or maybe a B&B, and I'd bring back fresh fish from my trips out in the boat. We liked Cornwall - who doesn't? - or Devon, and we had a look round at a few places. All I needed now was my replacement knees, and the world would be our oyster.

Two things got in the way of that.

I hadn't seen either of them coming.

I came home from work to find a letter from my insurance company telling me my car insurance hadn't been paid. I asked Marg if she knew anything about it.

I've put all your money in Barclays Bank.
Oh?
And mine in the Coventry.
What do you mean?

I'm leaving.
What?
I'm moving out.
Oh.
I've found a place...
Right.
And I'm moving out Saturday.

Was it a blow? Yes. But I just had to get on with it. There was no nastiness, and nobody else involved. It were just one of them things. We'd been through a hell of a lot over the past few years, and it just wore out the fabric of what we had. Marg asked if I knew anybody who'd got a van to help her move. I didn't, and who would I trust to do that anyway? So I borrowed a mate's van, loaded all her stuff up, drove her to her new house, and that were that.

I told Marg she'd always be welcome to come back and see the dogs whenever she wanted. Even if - at some point in the future - we weren't talking to each other for some reason, I'd never ever stop her from seeing the dogs. And then I drove back to my house.

That was blow number one. Blow number two was very different when it came, but it was every bit as bad.

It was 2014, and I had a job driving a tracked machine on a landfill site. It had been away to have new tracks fitted, and when they brought it back, I drove it off the low-loader. Everyone nodded happily and said *OK, off you go.*

I clunked my waist seatbelt into place, put the machine in high gear, started motoring off across the tip, and

BANG!

four 1" bolts sheared off. The machine shed one of its tracks, and that jammed the machine and stopped it dead.

The waist seat belt didn't hold me in place. I was shot forward, and whipped back. The pain was incredible. I knew this was bad - I couldn't move. My colleagues got me out of the cab, put me in a car, and drove me to the local hospital.

At this point I have to advise you that if ever anyone you know has a spinal injury, dragging them out of a cab and taking them to hospital in a car really isn't the best course of action. Keeping them as still as possible and bringing the professionals to them - like when I landed on my head in Stockport - is the right course of action. Everyone involved meant well, and they were trying to get me medical attention as quickly as possible, but when we got to the hospital the staff were furious. I was immediately put on a board, with my head and my limbs strapped so I couldn't move, and they sent me off to X-ray.

The news was bad. My spinal cord was crushed.

The force of the accident had caused one vertebra to slide across another and the result was there was a good chance I'd never walk again. I can't begin to tell you how hard a thing that is to hear.

I'd spent my whole life being active - playing football, being a wrestler, working physical jobs - I'd had the band fitted and endured the operations to re-fit my skin so I could rebuild my health, and now... this.

They fed me painkillers, assessed me and the injury, and sent me home. They knew they'd need to operate, but while I was waiting for them to set a date for that I spent two months at home, lying on the bed, waiting.

I can't tell you how difficult that was. Two months staring at the ceiling, wondering if I'd ever walk again. Finally they got in touch. They were going to drill away the bone to release the spinal cord and the sciatic nerve. The hope was this would relieve the pain, but the surgeon didn't want to promise anything more than that. He told me straight that I might never never walk again, because when a spinal cord's been crushed it doesn't ever open up properly again.

He warned me that while I might be able to walk after the operation, he thought I'd always drag one leg. He couldn't be sure, though. There was a chance I'd end up in a wheelchair. That was the worst outcome, getting back to being fully active was unlikely, and dragging one leg was probably what my future held. It was good doctoring. He was telling me straight. He said *I'll do my best, and I don't know what I can do till I open it up. Until then I don't know what it's going to be like in there.*

Afterwards, as I recovered on a hospital ward, the surgeon came to see me. He told me my spinal cord and been well and truly squashed.

Whether it'll come back... I can't say.

I came out of hospital on two crutches.

Marg picked me up and took me home. Yes, we'd split up, but she still took me home and cared for me, and I'll always be thankful for that. I needed a lot of care. Marg moved in for a while, till I could get about a bit, and then she moved back to her place. Even then, she still come round every day to look after me. I wouldn't have got through without that help, because – apart from visits to hospital for physio appointments – I didn't leave the house for eighteen months.

It was a dark, dark time.

I had two mental breakdowns in that eighteen months. The first was down to thinking how I might never walk without crutches again, might never be able to earn a living – the physio at hospital didn't seem to be helping at all, and I hated being reliant on Marg. The second breakdown was when I got a letter from work saying they couldn't pay me any more.

I went into meltdown. Things were difficult already – how would I cope without any money coming in? Marg had gone out shopping, so I couldn't talk this through with her. Instead, I rang the DSS and spoke to a woman there.

I told her what had happened and she said *I'll have to put you through to another department. They deal with that.* So, she put me through. I explained again. They put me through to someone else, and I had to explain again. And so it went on. In the finish I'd been round five people and I ended up back talking to the same woman I started with.

I couldn't cope. This was the straw that broke the camel's back (not the best turn of phrase in the circumstances, but there you go) and all the frustration and fear and anger I'd kept bottled up just spilled out. I threw the phone up in the air, howled and screamed, and tore at myself. By the time Marg came back from the shops I'd ripped all the skin off my arms. There were blood everywhere and I was just lying there, crying.

Marg rang the doctors. He said the surgery was shutting. She told him *You are not shutting till I get there!* and drove me over. The doctor took one look at me, and phoned the Crisis Team. By the time we got home, they were already waiting. They took all my tablets off me so I couldn't overdose – my mental health were so bad, they considered this a possibility – and from then on they came in each day to give me the tablets I needed at the time I needed them. And for the next three weeks I had to go to a place in Nuneaton for counselling.

Much as I hated admitting it, the impact of what had happened and the fear of being immobile had sent me round the twist.

Crochet

Did that counselling help? Yes, it did. Absolutely. The other people I met there were in the same situation as me, and learning you weren't alone, or having someone who'd been in the same place tell you how they'd got through, how they dealt with the fear, that hit home a lot more than some kind words from someone who could finish talking and stroll out of the room without a second thought.

Apart from the counselling, though, I still didn't go out. The doctors sent a woman round to encourage me. She told me I had to go out, I told her I didn't want to. So she asked me what I'd like to learn.

I had a list - although I didn't see how it would help me start going out. In no particular order, I wanted to learn how to work my computer properly, how to crochet, and how to tie flies for fly fishing. She said *OK, leave it with me.*

Maybe three days later she comes back and says, *Right, I cannot find anywhere at all for you to learn to tie flies, but I've found you a computer course, and I've found you where you can learn crochet. Just ring this number.*

So I did as I was told, and rang the number.

This lady - Mrs Smith it was - answered the phone, I told her I wanted to learn crochet, and she said *Yeah, come along on Tuesday night and we'll show you.*

I did. I went to the address she gave me, opened the door, and everyone in the class - bar me - was women. They weren't all old women, although a lot of them were older than me. Mrs Smith started learning me how to crochet. I loved it. I picked it up quick, and in no time at all I was crocheting mats, doilies, all that kind of thing. I was having a laugh, too, and I realised I'd forgotten how to have a laugh.

Little by little, things got better.

I started getting about on crutches, and a little after that I finally got my knees replaced. I'd been living with the pain of them for years - it was twenty years since I'd been to the doctors and he'd told me they were just bone grinding on bone - and although the days after the operation were painful, the relief that came after that was unbelievable. It took about six weeks, if that, to recover from each knee op, because I done my exercises.

Why?

Because I wanted to walk again. It was that simple. So I bought one of them big gym balls, and I'd sit on it three or four times a day and do my exercises. Rocking backwards and forwards so my knee was bending a bit more and a bit more and a bit more.

I should have had six visits to the knee clinic after my op, but when I went along the second time the doctor told me

Look, you can bend your knee better than me. There's no need for you to come back.

That was a result. A guy who'd been in for a knee op at the same time as me didn't do his exercises, and I seen him at the knee clinic later, and he still couldn't bend his knee. I'd say this to anybody – if you're having your knees done, do your exercises. It'll make all the difference.

Six months after the op on the first knee, I had the other one done. They don't like doing them together – though I do know people who've had them both done at the same time – because if you've got one good knee, you've got something you can rely on while you're getting the other one back up to scratch.

As my confidence and my mobility improved, I started going to my own physio. I had to pay for it myself, but it was money well spent, because she worked wonders. Over time she got me off the crutches onto walking with two sticks, which was amazing – the doctors had told me I might never walk again, remember? – and some months after that, thanks to her, I got to a point where I could walk with the aid of just one stick. Sometimes, now, I don't even use that.

Don't be fooled into thinking this was easy, just because it worked out. Getting through all this was a long haul, and – looking back – it was a terrible time in my life.

Without Marg, and the crisis team, and the counselling and the friends I made there, and Mrs Smith's crochet group and the friends I made there, who knows how things would have turned out? They helped me when I needed it, supported me when I didn't see a way forward, and gave me time to rebuild my life.

I'll always be grateful to them for that.

Now, I was walking again, even if I had to use a stick sometimes. On top of that, I had two new knees. The pain I'd lived with for years, all the way through having my gastric band, and through all those operations, was gone. You might think I'd feel a bit like the bionic man after all this.

Truth is I look a bit like a road map. With all the scars.

I knew I'd done really well, considering they'd told me after the accident that I'd never walk again. I didn't know it yet, but soon I'd get the opportunity to do even better.

Back In The Ring

After the accident, while I'd still been on crutches, I'd bumped into a wrestler called Mad Dog Maxx - Matt Powell, from the Black Country - at a seminar I'd done with Nigel Hanmore over in Rushall in October 2016. A year later, I met him again at the Leeds wrestling re-union. He had a proposition.

How would I feel about doing a manager's job?

I thought about it. And tried not to bite his hand off. *Yeah,* I said, *I wouldn't mind.* I missed wrestling, and while I couldn't see myself ever getting back in the ring again, this was a chance for me to make use of my years of expertise, and him to tap into it. We agreed I'd give it a go, once I felt up to it. Matt said he wasn't quite sure who he'd put me with yet, but whoever it was would a good lad, a good wrestler who'd benefit from that extra bit of guidance.

I spoke to Matt again when he did a show in Nuneaton, a month or so later. A month or so after that, when I was off my crutches, and getting around on one stick, I got in touch with Matt and told him

I'm ready now.

I drove over to Darlaston, where Matt ran his wrestling school, and he introduced me to Venom. He said *I think you'll help him a lot.* Well, me and Venom got on like a house on fire. He was a villain, and I'd been a villain, and I started doing the manager's job for him, and I loved it.

He got better and better, and I was getting a little bit more involved, and a little bit more involved... and a little bit more...

And I knew what was coming. I knew I needed to have a conversation with Matt. So one day I sat down with him and told him straight

I need to wrestle.
You can't.
I can, and I'm gunna.

He thinks for a few moments.

Are you sure?
Yes. I need to do it.

That was it decided, right there. Not everyone thought it was a good idea, though. When I'd told a couple of my old wrestling mates, Ron Marino and Pete Leplaque, that I was going to start doing the manager's job they both said I was crazy - *What do you want to get back doing that for?* - and now, when I told them I was going to wrestle again, they shook their heads and said my mum must have dropped me on my head when I was a baby, because I was going to kill myself, sure as eggs was eggs.

It's fair to say they weren't entirely positive, but that wasn't going to stop me. Nor did telling Alison the physio, who went a bit quiet, paused, and then said she couldn't say that this was a good idea, but I was a grown man and she supposed I knew the risks, and that she'd seen how much happier I was since I'd started being involved with wrestling again. But, really, it wasn't a good idea.

Over the next few months, every show we had, me and Venom kept chasing Matt for a match. The punters loved it. Venom would finish a match, I'd jump in the ring with him, and the pair of us would shout Matt out. He'd disappear. He just wouldn't get in the ring with us.

Then we done a show in Darlaston Town Hall. Venom had been on, I can't remember who with, and he'd beat 'em, and I was in the ring and on the mic, calling Matt out. Venom was outside the ring. I told him

You know what you've got to do now.

He says, *Yes, Boss.* He goes through the curtains to the backstage, and the next thing you hear is Elise - that's Matt's missus - screaming. Venom drags her out, pulls her down the steps by the scruff of her hair, and chucks her in the ring with me. I picks her up, hits her twice, and corners her. By this time, Venom's back in the ring. He corners me into her, and she drops down like she's dead.

I just stood with my foot on her. People were all round the ring, calling us women beaters, baying for blood. Matt comes running in with a chair, we leap out, and make our way through the crowd to the room where we do the training. The room is going absolutely crazy. Matt takes the mic as we're walking away, says

Venom, I want you in this ring! Daley, I want you to do a comeback! Meet me in a tag match. Here. Darlaston. You two have messed with my family, and you have got my attention.

Matt told us later he'd never seen the crowd that bad, that riled up. Even at the end of the night, he sent someone along to us in the training room and said we weren't to come back and help take the ring down, the crowd were still going mad.

He put the show on sale that night, and within two hours he'd sold all the VIPs and the front rows out. Completely. It were that good. We did a little pop-up show the following night, and they were still calling me and Venom woman beaters, twenty-four hours on. As soon as we walked in the room, they hated us. By the time the show came round in November, it had sold out and he had to open the balcony.

It was like old times, that hatred. It's what happens when you do your job. I always say, when you get that sort of thing, you've done your job right.

And that night in January 2018 when I got back in the ring as a wrestler – all those years after my first professional show in Brent – with me and Venom, villains and heels the pair of us, against Matt the blue-eye who's got the whole crowd rooting for him... I looked round the room, at all this faces screaming at us, wanting to see us get beaten and battered, and I knew.

There's nowhere else in the world I'd rather be.

Ever.

with Venom

all good management needs a horseshoe

Postscript

And if this was a Hollywood film, that's where we might end it. With me, back in the ring for the first time in years, putting my new knees and my lucky-to-be-in-one-piece spinal cord through their paces, and loving every minute of it.

And I did, and I do. To this day I say Matt gave me my life back. Because without him giving me a route back into wrestling, I'd have gone mad, sitting staring at four walls. I'm a few years older now, and I've got one or two health issues – I had a pacemaker fitted in 2019, as if enough of me hadn't been replaced already – and that means getting in the ring is that little bit harder each time. We had the pandemic, too, which stopped everything for a year or more, and where we lost one of Matt's young wrestlers, Cam Wellington who was a natural villain and had a real future in the sport.

I still get in the ring when I can. And when I'm not doing that I help Matt with the adults' training, and with the kids' class. I love it. I just love it. I feel as if I'm putting something back into what I love doing. There's going to come a time when I can't wrestle, but even then, I hope I can still do the training. Seeing the kids' faces when you show them a move, it's brilliant. Nothing beats it.

I'm a season ticket holder at Leicester Tigers, and if they're at home I go along with Ron Marino and Pete Leplaque, and the three of us sit together and talk about wrestling, and how it was, and how it is now, and how it's changed. And we watch a bit of rugby. They've both seen how I've changed since I started wrestling again. *We're glad you've done it, Mac.* They were worried for me, at the start, and I understand that. Being like that shows they're true friends. We talk about wrestling, watch the rugby, and have a bit of banter. You'll always find that wrestlers have got a different sense of humour from any-one else. We talk to each other different. People will hear us talking and look at us as much as to say *You shouldn't have said that to him!* But we know it's just banter.

Ron's seventy-nine. Pete's eighty-three. I've brought Ron with me to the wrestling a couple of times, and the second time, at the interval I went and sat with him, and he said *In all these years since I packed up wrestling* – and he packed up before I started, Ron did – *in all these years, I've never bothered before. But tonight, standing by that ring and looking at it, I got itchy feet, I wanted to get back in it.*

I made a couple of good friends out of the counselling, who I still speak to now. I still do my crochet. And a bit of knitting. After lockdown I got one of the women in the class to learn me how to do lace. At first, I could just about follow what she told me. Now, I'm making lace bookmarks, and surprising us both. Learning by doing, like I always do.

I've finally started tying flies, too. I found videos on YouTube guiding you through how to do it, and I had a go, and I've tied some lovely flies ready for fly-fishing. I'll be off in Rutland this weekend, trying out some of these flies I've tied. Maybe I'll catch something. I think that'll be the ultimate buzz, catching a trout on a fly that you've tied yourself, because you've convinced the trout that it's real. That's a proper test. We'll see how it goes.

Whatever happens, whatever's round the corner, I'll do what I've always done. I'll give it my best shot, I'll have a laugh, and I'll give it my all.

I've never been a person who does anything by halves.

And I've always, always, always been a wrestler.

Ignite Books is a small, independent publisher. This book is the latest in our series which we hope puts fresh, thought-provoking, entertaining writing before a new audience. We have a lot of fun doing this, but we also survive on a shoestring budget and a lot of graft. So, if you've enjoyed this book, please tell your friends about us.

You can also find us on Twitter, so drop by and say hello. And to learn more about what we do, buy more copies of this book, or shop for our other publications, just visit our website at ignitebooks.co.uk

Thank you.

Independent bookshops are wonders. Each and every one run by people passionate about books and the reading of them. Please support them when you buy, and help keep your high street thriving. Pop in and visit them, or do it from the comfort of your own home via either of these websites:

www.bookshop.org
www.hive.co.uk